SEVERE
COMPASSION

THE GOSPEL ACCORDING TO
THE OLD TESTAMENT

*A series of studies on the lives
of Old Testament characters, written for
laypeople and pastors, and designed to
encourage Christ-centered reading, teaching,
and preaching of the Old Testament*

IAIN M. DUGUID
Series Editor

SEVERE COMPASSION

THE GOSPEL ACCORDING TO
NAHUM

GREGORY D. COOK

P&R
P U B L I S H I N G
P.O. BOX 817 • PHILLIPSBURG • NEW JERSEY 08865-0817

Library of Congress Cataloging-in-Publication Data

Names: Cook, Gregory D., 1972- author.
Title: Severe compassion : the gospel according to Nahum / Gregory D. Cook.
Description: Phillipsburg : P&R Publishing, 2016. | Series: The Gospel according to the Old Testament | Includes bibliographical references and index.
Identifiers: LCCN 2015043790| ISBN 9781629951737 (pbk.) | ISBN 9781629951744 (epub) | ISBN 9781629951751 (mobi)
Subjects: LCSH: Bible. Nahum--Criticism, interpretation, etc. | Typology (Theology)
Classification: LCC BS1625.52 .C66 2016 | DDC 224/.9406--dc23
LC record available at http://lccn.loc.gov/2015043790

To Jesus

Who came down from heaven
Who restrains and conquers all his enemies
Who enabled his servants to break down the gates of hell
Who provides all that his children need
Who shepherds his people
Who judges injustice
Who redeems his people from slavery
Who seeks and saves the lost
Who broke the power of Satan
And so fulfills the book of Nahum

CONTENTS

SERIES FOREWORD

The New Testament is in the Old concealed;
the Old Testament is in the New revealed.
—Augustine

C oncerning this salvation, the prophets who
prophesied about the grace that was to be
yours searched and inquired carefully, inquir-
ing what person or time the Spirit of Christ in them
was indicating when he predicted the sufferings of
Christ and the subsequent glories. It was revealed
to them that they were serving not themselves but
you, in the things that have now been announced to
you through those who preached the good news to
you by the Holy Spirit sent from heaven, things into
which angels long to look. (1 Peter 1:10–12)

"Moreover, some women of our company amazed
us. They were at the tomb early in the morning, and
when they did not find his body, they came back
saying that they had even seen a vision of angels,
who said that he was alive. Some of those who were
with us went to the tomb and found it just as the
women had said, but him they did not see." And
he said to them, "O foolish ones, and slow of heart
to believe all that the prophets have spoken! Was
it not necessary that the Christ should suffer these
things and enter into his glory?" And beginning with
Moses and all the Prophets, he interpreted to them

in all the Scriptures the things concerning himself.
(Luke 24:22–27)

The prophets searched. Angels longed to see. And the disciples didn't understand. But Moses, the Prophets, and all the Old Testament Scriptures had spoken about it—that Jesus would come, suffer, and then be glorified. God began to tell a story in the Old Testament, the ending of which the audience eagerly anticipated. But the Old Testament audience was left hanging. The plot was laid out, but the climax was delayed. The unfinished story begged for an ending. In Christ, God has provided the climax to the Old Testament story. Jesus did not arrive unannounced; his coming was declared *in advance* in the Old Testament—not just in explicit prophecies of the Messiah, but also by means of the stories of all the events, characters, and circumstances in the Old Testament. God was telling a larger, overarching, unified story. From the account of creation in Genesis to the final stories of the return from exile, God progressively unfolded his plan of salvation. And the Old Testament account of that plan always pointed in some way to Christ.

AIMS OF THIS SERIES

The Gospel According to the Old Testament series was begun by my former professors, Tremper Longman and Al Groves, to whom I owe an enormous personal debt of gratitude. I learned from them a great deal about how to recognize the gospel in the Old Testament. I share their deep conviction that the Bible, both Old and New Testaments, is a unified revelation of God and that its thematic unity is found in Christ. This series of studies will continue to pursue their initial aims:

- to lay out the pervasiveness of the revelation of Christ in the Old Testament

- to promote a Christ-centered reading of the Old Testament
- to encourage Christ-centered preaching and teaching from the Old Testament

These volumes are written primarily for pastors and laypeople, not scholars. They are designed in the first instance to serve the church, not the academy.

My hope and prayer remain the same as Tremper and Al's: that this series will continue to encourage the revival of interest in the Old Testament as a book that constantly points forward to Jesus Christ, to his sufferings and the glories that would follow.

IAIN M. DUGUID

FOREWORD

Writing a book for modern people about the prophetic book of Nahum is not a task for the faint
of heart! I commend Greg Cook for devoting his
time and energy to studying Nahum and for sharing the
fruit of that study with all of us. It is a great and undeserved
privilege for me to write the foreword for this book.

My husband Al was, along with Tremper Longman, the
coeditor of this series from 1999 until his death in 2007. Al
loved the Old Testament and was excited and passionate
about the belief that every part of it points to Jesus. The
variety and beauty of the ways in which it does so enthralled
him. He devoted his life—and this series—to helping others
see Jesus in the Old Testament.

Greg was Al's student. I see Al's influence and hear his
voice (sometimes even his exact words!) throughout this
volume. I know he would be very pleased with this book
and proud of Greg's work in producing it. It combines so
many things that Al taught, stressed, and valued. Among
them:

- a profound, life-shaping fear of God and a love of
  his Word,
- the hard work of digging deep into the text, including close, careful work with the Hebrew, yielding
  insights that are sometimes lost in translation
  (e.g., chapter 5's discussion of verbs' person, gender, and number),
- a thorough familiarity with and appreciation of
  scholarly writings about the text, accompanied by
  a discerning eye that allows one to benefit from

all that is valuable in such writings while also recognizing, evaluating, and critiquing any problematic presuppositions,

- an awareness of the details of the author's world and of the cultural and historical background in/to/against which he was writing,
- an appreciation of the beauty of the writing and the literary skill of the author, an ear that is fine-tuned to hear echoes of other texts, and alert attention paid to how the author used those other texts,
- the willingness to *s-i-t* for a long time with the text and to *l-i-s-t-e-n* to it carefully and humbly, with an open ear and mind, to let it speak and teach *us* rather than presuming that we already know what it has to say or that its message has long since been pinpointed and archived,
- and eyes to see and ears to hear the Holy Spirit pointing to Christ in the text. (This above all was Al's heartbeat.)

All of the above Greg does in this book. He has done the hard work of digging into the Hebrew text, he has gleaned insights from scholars and learned about the world and time in which Nahum wrote, he has sat with and listened carefully and humbly to the text, he has seen and appreciated how it speaks about and points to Jesus, and he has then gone on to consider how its message speaks to us today as people in union with Christ. The result is a volume that is well worth reading, that makes Nahum accessible to us through Jesus, and that, I believe, will be a blessing to the church.

Elizabeth W. D. Groves
Lecturer in Old Testament
Westminster Theological Seminary

ACKNOWLEDGMENTS

I need to thank God before I do anything else. I am grateful for the opportunity to study Nahum. I am grateful for what I have learned, and I am grateful for the opportunity to share it. Much more importantly, I am grateful that God would send his Son to die for me.

Next, thanks go to my family. I wish to thank my wife, Kim. She is beautiful and amazing. We have been married for seventeen years, and every day I am thankful for her love. We have seven children. I am not sure how many of them knew what I was doing with my laptop all those hours. Each of them—Theodore, Anastasia, Eden, Caleb, Joshua, Noah, and Lily—make my life rich and full.

I would like to thank Iain Duguid for his endorsement of this project and for his willingness to lend his expertise to editing the book. I have used Dr. Duguid's commentaries for years in sermon preparation. I appreciate the opportunity now to work with him. Also, Amanda Martin at P&R Publishing quickly and capably answered all my questions. Thank you, Amanda.

I would also like to thank two former professors. Michael Kelly befriended me early in my Ph.D. studies, helped me immensely through the entire process, and supervised my dissertation on Nahum. Thank you, Mike, for all your work. The late J. Alan Groves spent much of his career in a dungeon-like basement of Westminster Theological Seminary developing Hebrew-language computer programs. I relied heavily on Al's software to do much of the research behind this book. Kim and I went to Israel in 2000 with a group led by Al and Libbie Groves, and they were wonderful hosts. I asked Libbie to write the foreword for this book, and she graciously agreed. For that I am also grateful.

CHAPTER ONE

JEALOUS LOVE (1:1–2)

Set me as a seal upon your heart,
as a seal upon your arm,
for love is strong as death,
jealousy is fierce as the grave. (Song 8:6)

M ost of us had at least one teacher whose strict rule of the classroom inspired fear. Apparently my grandmother was a legend in this regard—though she mostly gave me Oreos and told me how smart I was, so I did not find her intimidating. On the other hand, my seventh-grade English class was devoid of cookies and compliments; I cowered before my teacher. The many assignments in that class included memorizing a famous poem each week. As I think back on this experience, I find it ironic that my first attempts to understand literary beauty were driven by terror.

If you learned about poetry through academic pressure, I encourage you to pause now and ask God to give you eyes to see, ears to hear, and a heart to understand Nahum (Matt. 13:15). Nahum, like many portions of the Old Testament, is poetry. We must read it as poetry to grasp its message. To enjoy Nahum and find edification in it, we must read it carefully, noticing the nuances. Doing this requires a brief and painless return to poetry class.

Poets create literary art. They paint with words. Every aspect of a poem has its place and plays its part. The master poet brings the whole work together into an expressive masterpiece. Nahum created just such a masterpiece. All who study Hebrew poetry recognize the literary brilliance of this book. Over two hundred years ago, Robert Lowth wrote, "None of the minor prophets . . . seem to equal Nahum in boldness, ardour, and sublimity. His prophecy too forms a regular and perfect poem; the exordium is not merely magnificent, it is truly majestic."[1] These words still represent how critics view the literary expression in this book. As we study Nahum, we will examine how the book uses literary techniques to express its message.

THREE POETIC DEVICES

The first two verses of Nahum provide insight into the character of God as well as into the purpose of the prophecy. To understand this, we need first to discuss three aspects of poetry prevalent in Nahum: brevity, wordplay, and allusion. *Brevity* simply means that poetry uses fewer words than prose. Sentences are shorter. Poems communicate key details by means other than direct statement. This characteristic may be observed by scanning through the Old Testament. Most English versions indent the poetic portions. The lines are more compact in the indented sections. The brevity of Old Testament poetry warrants careful reading. What does the author say? What does he leave unsaid? In what subtle ways does he communicate to the reader? Perhaps no book of the Bible demands a more careful reading than Nahum; few books, if any, contain as many terse phrases and clauses as this one.

The next poetic device for us to consider, *wordplay*, occurs frequently in the Old Testament. One book on Hebrew poetry explains that in wordplay, "two words with similar sounds may occur in the same context, or one word may be used with two different meanings."[2] This concept is well known in kindergartens around the country. As children begin to develop their sense of humor, they quiz each other with puns. Every punch line in a children's joke book contains a double meaning. (Why is 6 afraid of 7? Because 7 8 9—it may take you a minute.) Wordplay occurs outside of humor as well. Many advertising slogans make a play on words. My aunt recently ordered bakery goodies for our family. They came in a box marked "Gifts in Good Taste." Old Testament authors also use wordplays, but they have a serious, theological purpose. These wordplays occur with great frequency in poetry; we will find a number of them in Nahum.

Allusion happens when an author wants the reader to recognize an unstated reference. I first realized the subtlety of allusion when I spent a summer in South Africa. When I watched American movies with South Africans, I found myself laughing at allusions that they completely missed. When a movie, book, or song uses an allusion, those who do not recognize the allusion usually do not realize that they have missed something. Nahum contains many such allusions. These are subtle references either to previous biblical prayers and prophecies or to Assyrian ideology. Since we have no personal experience with the Assyrian Empire and we do not know the Old Testament Scriptures nearly as well as Nahum's original audience, we are at a disadvantage in discerning these allusions.

AN ORACLE CONCERNING NINEVEH

The first words of Nahum identify the book as an oracle. Nahum uses a Hebrew word that refers to a specific type, or genre, of prophecy. All the prophetic passages described as oracles declare the historical fulfillment of previous prophecies.[3] Since the first verse describes the entire book as an oracle, we know that Nahum's words will declare the fulfillment of promises spoken by earlier prophets.

The next two words establish the subject of this prophecy. The book concerns Nineveh, the capital city of the Assyrian Empire. Nineveh had not always been Assyria's capital. For most of Assyria's history, the city of Asshur filled this role. Nineveh was an ancient city mentioned in Genesis 10:11, but it had limited importance to Assyria for most of its history. Then a series of unexpected events changed the fate of Nineveh, making it the most formidable and feared city in the world for a brief period of time. First, Sargon II usurped the Assyrian throne from Shalmaneser V in 722 B.C. He proceeded to build a new capital in Dur-Sharrukin (modern Khorsabad) to consolidate his power. Second, Sargon died in battle. Since Assyrian kings rarely died in battle, this was seen as an evil omen. What compounded this disaster in the eyes of the Assyrians was that they believed his unburied spirit would haunt Dur-Sharrukin. This led to the third event. Sargon's son, Sennacherib, lost no time in establishing a new capital in Nineveh. In doing so, he greatly expanded and built up the city—using Israelite slaves and money. This ancient city devoted to the goddess Ishtar soon became the largest and most ostentatious city in the world. As rapidly as it had arisen, it would fall even more quickly—due to a prophet.

A VISION

The introductory verse also describes Nahum's oracle as "the book of the vision." The word "book" suggests that the book of Nahum originated as a written document rather than as a spoken message. The description "vision" explains why the scenes are so vivid. Apparently Nahum actually saw the events he described. The phrase "the book of the vision" puts Nahum in the same class as Revelation. John said that a loud voice told him, "'Write what you see

4

in a book and send it to the seven churches, to Ephesus and to Smyrna and to Pergamum and to Thyatira and to Sardis and to Philadelphia and to Laodicea.' Then I turned to see the voice that was speaking to me, and on turning I saw seven golden lampstands" (Rev. 1:11–12). Like John, Nahum recorded events that he had seen in his mind, but which had not yet happened in history.

INTRODUCING THE PROPHET

The final words of Nahum 1:1 introduce our prophet. We know nothing about Nahum except for his name, hometown, and time period. In the Bible, names have purpose. The name-giver prophesied the outcome of the person's life. Some examples of this include Abraham ("father of many nations"), Peter ("rock"), and Jesus ("salvation"). Nahum's name means "comfort" or "compassion." His name strikes people as either fitting or ironic, depending on the perspective of the interpreter. Many people consider the name appropriate because his message brought relief to those who had suffered the brutality of Assyria. Others note the violent language in the book and suggest that Nahum's parents misnamed him. We will see later that Nahum's name fits this book in a number of ways, but the compassion proclaimed in the book does not conform to our expectations.

Nahum spoke a message of compassion, yet he hailed from Elkosh, a town named for God's hardness. The word *Elkosh* means "God is severe." We do not know this town's location. There are many theories. For instance, it has been suggested that Elkosh was renamed Capernaum when later inhabitants wanted to identify it as the hometown of Nahum. None of the theories regarding Elkosh's location have strong evidence to support them. We may conclude, however, that the town endured a catastrophe attributed to God's chastisement. The words "Nahum of Elkosh" form a fitting theological introduction to this book, which unites God's compassion and his severity.

We also know that Nahum's life experiences included suffering under the most malicious king in Assyria's history and the most atrocious king in the Davidic line. Unlike many Old Testament books, we can easily establish a range of possible dates for the book of Nahum. The discussion of Nahum's date will wait until chapter 5, but the entire range of possible dates falls during the reign of Ashurbanipal (668–627 B.c.). For reasons to be discussed later, Ashurbanipal has the dubious distinction of being the most vicious king in a long line of evil Assyrian rulers. Nahum also lived in the period of King Manasseh of Judah, who reigned approximately from 697 to 642 B.c. (2 Kings 21:1–18; 2 Chron. 33:1–20). Manasseh's gross wickedness against God and his subjects reached unthinkable levels. Nahum no doubt witnessed abominable deeds practiced by foreigners and kinsmen alike.

A JEALOUS GOD

After a brief introductory verse, Nahum begins by telling the reader that God is jealous. This short statement proclaims theological truth, but also makes an allusion. Nahum uses a specific Hebrew clause that occurs in only six other Old Testament passages (Ex. 20:5; 34:14; Deut. 4:24; 5:9; 6:15; Josh. 24:19). All six passages have two important themes in common. In each case, God establishes or renews his covenant with Israel. In each case, he also gives Israel a dire warning not to worship foreign gods.

Nahum begins his prophecy in this way in order to remind his readers of these warnings. God is jealous and will not permit his people to serve foreign gods. Unfortunately, the people of Nahum's time had done exactly that, with disastrous consequences. Isaiah 7—a famous prophecy of Jesus—tells the story. When King Ahaz ruled Judah, the king of Israel and the king of Syria united against him. God sent Isaiah to reassure Ahaz and strengthen his faith. In that encounter, Isaiah prophesied,

> The Lord himself will give you a sign. Behold, the virgin shall conceive and bear a son, and shall call his name Immanuel. He shall eat curds and honey when he knows how to refuse the evil and choose the good. For before the boy knows how to refuse the evil and choose the good, the land whose two kings you dread will be deserted. (Isa. 7:14–16)

Ahaz did not honor God's covenant or trust his message. Instead he "sent messengers to Tiglath-pileser king of Assyria, saying, 'I am your servant and your son. Come up and rescue me from the hand of the king of Syria and from the hand of the king of Israel, who are attacking me'" (2 Kings 16:7). This act of faithlessness resulted in Judah submitting to foreign kings and gods; it also brought one hundred years of brutal tyranny upon the people of Judah. In a few words, Nahum has set his prophecy in the context of God's covenant with Judah, Judah's rejection of that covenant, Judah's submission to Assyrian deities, and God's resulting curse: "You shall not bow down to them or serve them, for I the LORD your God am a jealous God, visiting the iniquity of the fathers on the children to the third and the fourth generation of those who hate me" (Ex. 20:5).

AN AVENGING GOD

Nahum 1:2 proceeds to give one of the clearest statements of God's vengeance in the Bible. Many people cringe at this aspect of God's character. Undoubtedly this contributes to the scarcity of references to the book of Nahum in worship services. However, we cannot afford to ignore or avoid any aspect of God's character. "All Scripture is breathed out by God and profitable for teaching, for reproof, for correction, and for training in righteousness" (2 Tim. 3:16). We read the Bible to know God. He has told us about himself. We will not know God if we refuse to listen to his self-description. Those who will not allow the Bible to describe God do not worship the God of the Bible; they worship a god of their own making. Isaiah says that such a person "fashions a god or casts an idol that is profitable for nothing" (Isa. 44:10). Whether the idol is fashioned with tools or theology, it is a false god.

Nahum 1:2 tells us three times that the God of the Bible takes vengeance on his enemies. Some may object that Nahum's description speaks only of how God acted in the Old Testament. This objection deserves consideration. In the Old Testament, we find commands for Israel to execute God's justice by killing people (e.g., Num. 31:17). In the New Testament, the church has no such authority. A closer examination, though, shows that Nahum 1:2 speaks as the New Testament speaks: God alone has the right of vengeance. It is his to dispense, not ours.

According to Nahum 1:2, "The LORD is a jealous and avenging God; the LORD is avenging and wrathful; the LORD takes vengeance on his adversaries and keeps wrath for his enemies." In Hebrew, the language of the Old Testament, the doubling of a word shows emphasis or intensity. In rare cases, a word appears three times to give it extreme emphasis. For instance, the angelic host cry out, "Holy, holy, holy is the LORD of hosts; the whole earth is full of his glory!" (Isa. 6:3). Nahum 1:2 three times uses the name Yahweh with the verb *avenge*. Between the second and third assertions of Yahweh's vengeance, Nahum inserts a statement that wrath belongs to God. Therefore, Nahum's prophecy begins with an intensive statement of God's jealousy, vengeance, and wrath.

At this point, we need to ask whether these characteristics of God can be reconciled with the profound statements of love and grace that are so deeply embedded in the New Testament. The biblical answer is that God's jealousy, vengeance, and wrath may not be separated from his love and grace. They belong to the same God because they are essential to each other.

NAHUM AND NEW TESTAMENT LOVE

To show this, we may compare Nahum 1:2 with Jesus' words:

> You shall love the Lord your God with all your heart and with all your soul and with all your mind. This is the great and first commandment. And a second is like it: You shall love your neighbor as yourself. (Matt. 22:37–39)

First, we need to note that Jesus went on to say, "On these two commandments depend all the Law and the Prophets" (Matt. 22:40). Jesus claims that these two statements are consistent with the teaching of all the prophets. Does he overstate the case to make a point, sidestepping verses like Nahum 1:2? No, he does not. In saying that we must love our neighbors as ourselves, Jesus quoted part of Leviticus 19:18. The entire verse reads, "You shall not take vengeance or bear a grudge against the sons of your own people, but you shall love your neighbor as yourself: I am the LORD." Leviticus 19:18 gives a negative command and a positive one. When the Bible issues a command, it also explains the means by which we may obey the command. In Leviticus 19:18, the power not to take vengeance and the power to love our neighbor come from knowing that God is God. While Leviticus commands us to "not take vengeance," Nahum 1:2 declares that "the LORD takes vengeance." Nahum and Leviticus use the same Hebrew phrase. We noted before that Nahum declares that wrath belongs to God. Vengeance belongs to him too. Leviticus and Nahum teach the same message: vengeance is God's right. Jesus forbade his followers to take vengeance on their enemies, but he never denied that God would judge. The apostle Paul summarizes how Leviticus, Nahum, and Jesus all affirm this doctrine when he writes,

> Beloved, never avenge yourselves, but leave it to the wrath of God, for it is written, "Vengeance is mine, I will repay, says the Lord." To the contrary, "if your enemy is hungry, feed him; if he is thirsty, give him something to drink; for by so doing you will heap burning coals on his head." Do not be overcome by evil, but overcome evil with good. (Rom. 12:19–21)

Romans 12 commands us to love and forgive our enemies. It proceeds to instruct us to demonstrate this love and forgiveness through outward actions. It also explains the power by which we may love and forgive: faith that God will avenge. We are to trust that God sees and that God will repay. Nahum, Leviticus, Jesus, and Paul all agree that vengeance belongs to God. If we choose to ignore God's justice because it makes us uncomfortable, we also lose the power to love our enemies.

JEALOUSY AND VENGEANCE AS EXPRESSIONS OF GOD'S LOVE

Enabling us to love our enemies is not the most important aspect of God's vengeance, though. If we jettison God's vengeance in an effort to safeguard his love, we end up creating a God who does not love. The Song of Solomon says, "Love is strong as death, jealousy is fierce as the grave" (8:6). God's desire for his people requires an exclusive relationship. God's fierce love for us kindles his jealousy when we give our hearts, souls, and minds to other loves. God's love also ignites his wrath against any who would draw us away from him. If God did not care when our hearts are far from him (Isa. 29:13) or when we adulterously give our hearts to the world (James 4:4), he would not love us. If God did not care that the world, the flesh, and the Devil attempt to seduce us away from him (Eph. 2:2–3), he would not love us. If God could watch us suffer grievous injustice without punishing evil (Deut. 32:35–36), he would not love us. The notion of a love without jealousy and vengeance cannot survive a thorough biblical examination. It is a concept lacking passion or power. It is apathy masquerading as virtue. When Adam sinned, humanity's relationship with God was ripped apart. Each and every one of us, at the deepest level of our soul, longs for a restored and passionate relationship with our Father who made us. Apathy cannot fill our deepest longing: to be in a right, passionate relationship with our Creator.

We know that we want God to love us passionately. We also know that God's passionate love threatens our other loves (Luke 14:26). To enjoy his exclusive love, we must surrender all other loves. We must die to the world and to our own flesh (Gal. 2:19–20). For many people, that price is just too high. We search for some way that we can have God love us while we still love the world. If that requires reinventing the God of the Bible, then so be it. Let us be honest. Our objections to God's vengeance and justice do not come primarily from trying to defend God's character. They come from trying to safeguard our standing as good Christians while we live lives devoted to a world that hates God. Revelation 19:7 says, "Let us rejoice and exult and give him the glory, for the marriage of the Lamb has come, and his Bride has made herself ready." Christ has a jealous love for his people. He became man, lived a perfect life, and "for the joy that was set before him endured the cross, despising the shame" (Heb. 12:2). His love for his bride drove him to endure even the rejection of God the Father

11

(Mark 15:34). He did this to gain a bride "without spot or blemish" (2 Peter 3:14). We dare not take jealousy and vengeance out of this love, for in both the Old Testament and the New Testament, God's love requires jealousy and vengeance.

GOD'S COMFORT

Before leaving Nahum 1:1–2, we need to examine one more allusion. These two verses unveil the purpose of the prophecy through an allusion to Isaiah 1:24, which ends with, "Ah, I will get relief from my enemies and avenge myself on my foes." Although the ESV uses fourteen words in this quote, the original Hebrew text contains only five. Each of these five Hebrew words appears in Nahum. The first word, "Ah," occurs in Nahum 3:1, where most English versions translate it as "Woe!" The remaining four Hebrew words all occur in Nahum 1:1–2. Most notably, the word that the ESV translates as "relief" is the root word for Nahum's name. Less than a century before, Isaiah had recorded God's desire for a purified people. God had used Assyria to chasten Judah as a means of that purification. Yet Assyria went well beyond God's mandate. Assyrian officials mocked God (2 Kings 18:19–35) and forced Judah to submit to Assyrian gods. Now Nahum declares the end of the Assyrian affliction and God's intention to avenge this injustice. The allusion to Isaiah 1:24 reveals that the purpose of the book of Nahum matches the ultimate purpose of all things: God's glory. Nahum's name fits his life because his words bring God comfort.

GOD-CENTERED CHRISTIANITY

This exposes a common error in our Christianity. We tend to read the Bible as if it focuses on us. It does not.

The primary concern of the Bible is that God would be glorified. The primary reason for missions and evangelism is not to save people from hell, as important as that is. The primary reason to abandon all to tell others about Christ is that he might receive glory. The ultimate purpose of rescuing sinners is that people from "every nation and tribe and language and people" (Rev. 14:6) would exalt Christ. In the end, every knee will "bow, in heaven and on earth and under the earth, and every tongue confess that Jesus Christ is Lord, to the glory of God the Father" (Phil. 2:10–11). The Bible calls us to give our lives now, so that this worship will happen voluntarily—being done by people who have been cleansed of their sin and therefore love Christ.

Likewise, Nahum did not prophesy primarily to bring Judah comfort. He desired to bring comfort to God. Nahum's allusion to Isaiah 1:24 reminds us how seriously God views sin. It also reinforces how deeply he loves his people. God's powerful love and his hatred of sin create a conflict as he deeply desires intimacy with us while finding the sin in us revolting. The Bible tells the story of God's plan of redemption—how he could still love and be in union with a sin-soaked people (1 John 4:10). The book of Nahum focuses on one specific part of that story: God's vengeance against those who have drawn his beloved's affections away from him. Nahum's words point forward to the day when God's vengeance against all rivals will be complete. In that day, God's promise will be fulfilled:

> I will sprinkle clean water on you, and you shall be clean from all your uncleannesses, and from all your idols I will cleanse you. And I will give you a new heart, and a new spirit I will put within you. And I will remove the heart of stone from your flesh and give you a heart of flesh. And I will put my Spirit within you, and cause you to walk in my statutes and be careful to obey my rules. (Ezek. 36:25–27)

13

FOR FURTHER REFLECTION

1. Read Exodus 20:4–6; 34:12–15; Deuteronomy 4:23–28; 5:6–10; 6:13–15; Joshua 24:18–24. Note how seriously these passages treat idolatry. Discuss whether you have ever taken the warnings in these passages seriously. What would it look like to do so?
2. Read James 4:4–10 and 1 John 2:15–17. How do the Old Testament warnings about idolatry carry over for the New Testament church? What does idolatry look like in our lives and in our churches?
3. Read Psalm 109. There are many prayers in the Psalms that ask God to bring vengeance. Have you ever prayed for God's vengeance? How might an assurance that God will avenge allow you to forgive those whom you have not been able to forgive?
4. What areas of your life compete with God for your heart's affections? Please be honest. What do you desire most? What arouses your passions? Have you ever asked God to remove everything in your life that would steal away your love for him? If you have asked, what has happened? If you have not, are you willing to?

CHAPTER TWO

RESTORATION (1:3a)

He said to him the third time, "Simon, son of John, do
you love me?" Peter was grieved because he said to him
the third time, "Do you love me?" and he said to him,
"Lord, you know everything; you know that I love you."
Jesus said to him, "Feed my sheep." (John 21:17)

In the twentieth century, there were few places more
dangerous to confess Christ than China. The book *Jesus
Freaks* recounts the following story of one faithful man:
"In Mainland China, a sword was put to the chest of a
Christian. He was asked, 'Are you a Christian?' He answered
'Yes.' He would have been killed if an officer had not said,
'Free him; he is an idiot.' Someone asked him later, 'How
could you confess Christ with such courage?' He replied,
'I had read the story of Peter's denial of Jesus, and I did
not wish to weep bitterly.'"[1]

For every such story of someone standing firm, many
others speak of failure. The Bible tells both. Some of the
Bible's greatest triumphs of faith were followed by disastrous sin. How does God deal with us when we betray
him? Peter failed when Jesus most needed his companions.
Instead of having disciples on his right and his left when
Jesus entered his kingdom—which James and John had
requested (Mark 10:37)—Jesus died between two thieves
who joined the crowd in mockery (Matt. 27:44). Even

though Peter and the rest of the disciples had promised to die with Jesus (Matt. 26:35), he suffered alone. Instead of having his disciples witness for him, they fled and Peter denied him three times (Mark 14:72). Because of this failure and the shame that accompanied it, Peter needed restoration before he would be of any use to the church. John 21 records the painful process in which Jesus confronted Peter with his sin and commissioned him again.

ISRAEL'S PAST REBELLIONS

The book of Nahum performs a similar restoration for the nation of Judah. Like Peter, Judah buckled under fear and disowned God; Judah decided to submit to an evil king and evil gods. This decision had horrific consequences. How could God restore his unfaithful people so that they might once again serve him? Nahum addresses this question by quoting one of the most famous statements in the Old Testament: "The LORD is slow to anger and great in power, and the LORD will by no means clear the guilty" (Nah. 1:3a). This description abbreviates the words that God spoke to Moses after the Israelites worshiped the golden calf: "The LORD, the LORD, a God merciful and gracious, slow to anger, and abounding in steadfast love and faithfulness, keeping steadfast love for thousands, forgiving iniquity and transgression and sin, but who will by no means clear the guilty, visiting the iniquity of the fathers on the children and the children's children, to the third and the fourth generation" (Ex. 34:6–7).

It is important to note, however, that Nahum 1:3 does not directly quote Exodus 34. Instead, it uses Numbers 14:17–18, where Moses pleads,

And now, please let the power of the Lord be great as you have promised, saying, "The LORD is slow to anger and abounding in steadfast love, forgiv-

16

ing iniquity and transgression, but he will by no means clear the guilty, visiting the iniquity of the fathers on the children, to the third and the fourth generation."

Notice how Nahum 1:3 inserts Moses' assertion about God's great power (Num. 14:17) into God's own statement about being slow to anger (Num. 14:18). Nahum's reference to Exodus 34:6-7 by way of Numbers 14:17-18 causes readers to recall two disasters in Israel's history: the golden calf and the wilderness rebellion. In the first, Israel sinned by its actions, engaging in idolatrous revelry. In the second, Israel sinned by its inaction, failing to believe God and attack Canaan. By action and inaction, Israel proved faithless to the covenant.

JUDAH'S APOSTASY

By using this quotation at the beginning of the book, Nahum compares Judah's situation in the mid-seventh century B.C. to those past failures. The quotation makes two important theological points. It shows us the seriousness of Judah's sin, and it shows us the reason for God's mercy. To understand this, we must revisit Exodus 32-34 and Numbers 13-14. Exodus 32 relates that the Israelites grew impatient while Moses remained on Mount Sinai. They appealed to Aaron to make gods for them. Aaron took the gold that God had provided as they left Egypt (Ex. 12:35-36) and fashioned a golden calf for them to worship. They "worshiped it and sacrificed to it and said, 'These are your gods, O Israel, who brought you up out of the land of Egypt!'" (Ex. 32:8). These actions provoked God's anger so much that he told Moses, "Let me alone, that my wrath may burn hot against them and I may consume them, in order that I may make a great nation of you" (32:10).

Numbers 13–14 recounts similar events. God had miraculously delivered Israel out of Egypt. He had shown them his power and his glory, providing for their every need. When the time came to conquer Canaan, the people lost heart and rebelled against God, despite the pleadings of Moses, Aaron, Caleb, and Joshua. Again God announced his intention to "strike them with the pestilence and disinherit them" (Num. 14:12).

Let us pause here and ask, "What determines the seriousness of sin?" We make judgments every day, consciously and unconsciously, about the gravity of sins. The Bible provides the only reliable standard to answer that question. We often have a strong desire to dwell on the seriousness of sin in others while minimizing our own. Hence, Jesus asks, "Why do you see the speck that is in your brother's eye, but do not notice the log that is in your own eye?" (Matt. 7:3), and Paul says we "exchanged the truth about God for a lie" (Rom. 1:25). We cannot be trusted to evaluate our own actions honestly.

A person may object that all sin is equally serious and therefore that the question is invalid, since James declares all sin abhorrent and worthy of judgment (James 2:10). Yet the Westminster Shorter Catechism states, "Some sins in themselves, and by reason of several aggravations, are more heinous in the sight of God than others" (WSC 83), and Exodus 32–34 and Numbers 13–14 support this idea. In both passages, God's wrath threatens to annihilate Israel. The Bible teaches that God treats this form of rebellion as especially serious.

When we enter into covenant with God, receive the blessings of that covenant, and then worship what the world worships, we sin deeply. Israel committed this sin in Exodus 32. Israel again committed this sin in Numbers 13. Judah committed this sin when it chose Assyrian protection instead of faithfulness to God. We commit this sin when we find God boring and the world fascinating (1 John 2:15–16).

THE MEANS OF FORGIVENESS

This raises the question, "By what means may we find forgiveness and restoration?" How will Israel, Judah, and we survive God's wrath and be brought back into fellowship with him? Exodus, Numbers, and Nahum each answer that question with the same answer. Intercession by a righteous person allows God to forgive and restore. In Exodus 32, Moses intercedes for Israel:

> O LORD, why does your wrath burn hot against your people, whom you have brought out of the land of Egypt with great power and with a mighty hand? Why should the Egyptians say, 'With evil intent did he bring them out, to kill them in the mountains and to consume them from the face of the earth'? Turn from your burning anger and relent from this disaster against your people. Remember Abraham, Isaac, and Israel, your servants, to whom you swore by your own self, and said to them, "I will multiply your offspring as the stars of heaven, and all this land that I have promised I will give to your offspring, and they shall inherit it forever." (Ex. 32:11–13)

God relented because of Moses' prayer.

Why did this prayer prove effective? Let us consider three reasons. First, it came from a man who knew and walked with God. James 5:16 says, "The prayer of a righteous person has great power." Second, Moses prayed for the sake of God's glory. The Egyptians had seen God's power in the exodus. If God destroyed Israel, the Egyptians would misunderstand the exodus, and it would undermine their awe of God. Third, Moses based his prayer on God's word: previous promises made to Abraham, Isaac, and Jacob. The Bible assures us that "if we ask anything according to his will he hears us" (1 John 5:14). We know that our prayers conform to God's will if we pray God's word back to him.

Similarly, in Numbers 14 Moses begged God,

> Please let the power of the Lord be great as you have promised, saying, "The LORD is slow to anger and abounding in steadfast love, forgiving iniquity and transgression, but he will by no means clear the guilty, visiting the iniquity of the fathers on the children, to the third and the fourth generation." Please pardon the iniquity of this people, according to the greatness of your steadfast love, just as you have forgiven this people, from Egypt until now. (Num. 14:17–19)

Again, Moses' prayer brought an immediate reprieve from the announced judgment. Neither prayer, however, effected a full pardon. In Exodus 32, Moses descended the mountain, called forth the Levites, and commanded them to "kill his brother and his companion and his neighbor" (Ex. 32:27). God sent a plague on the people as well (32:35). In Numbers 14, the Lord announced that all those over twenty years of age would die in the wilderness because of their rebellion. To fully appease God's wrath would require a more effective intercession than Moses could provide.

DEUTERONOMY, JONAH, AND NAHUM

Having seen why Nahum quoted Numbers and Exodus, we will now examine the historical events that led up to Nahum's prophecy. When Nahum saw his vision, Judah was suffering as a vassal of the Neo-Assyrian Empire.[2] Although the Assyrian Empire had existed for well over a thousand years by this time, little of that history involved Israel and Judah. Jonah changed that.

To understand how Jonah brought Assyria into Israelite affairs, we need to start with a prophecy that Moses made long before Jonah lived. The book of Deuteronomy records Moses' instructions to Israel as they readied to enter the Promised

Land. Moses knew that he would soon die. He began by reminding the Israelites how God had been faithful to them. In Deuteronomy 5, Moses repeated the Ten Commandments and then proceeded in the following chapters to explain how these commandments applied to their future lives in Canaan. Then, in Deuteronomy 28, Moses explained that obedience to God's law would bring blessing, while disobedience would unleash curses. In the extensive section that details potential curses, Moses said, "If you are not careful to do all the words of this law that are written in this book, that you may fear this glorious and awesome name, the LORD your God, then the LORD . . . will scatter you among all peoples, from one end of the earth to the other, and there you shall serve other gods of wood and stone, which neither you nor your fathers have known" (Deut. 28:58–59, 64). God's word is true. It will come to pass. Israel did indeed fail to keep God's law, so God prepared a means by which Israel would be scattered "among all peoples, from one end of the earth to the other." This instrument was the Assyrian Empire.[3]

By considering Assyrian history and the biblical record, we may conclude that God used Jonah to transform Assyria from a failing state to an agent of God's justice. The book of Jonah does not give a date for Jonah's prophecy, but a passage in 2 Kings provides a general idea. Second Kings 14:25 says that King Jeroboam II "restored the border of Israel from Lebo-hamath as far as the Sea of the Arabah, according to the word of the LORD, the God of Israel, which he spoke by his servant Jonah the son of Amittai, the prophet." Since Jeroboam II reigned from 793 to 753 B.C., we know that Jonah prophesied during a pivotal time for the Assyrian Empire.

In the mid-eighth century B.C., Assyria was failing. A series of natural disasters had plagued the nation. The economy struggled, and vassals rebelled. In 745 B.C., Tiglath-pileser III orchestrated a successful *coup d'état*. For the next eighteen years, Tiglath-pileser led Assyrian armies in constant conquest. By the time of his death in 727 B.C.,

Assyria stood as the largest empire the world had ever seen. Besides using his military brilliance, Tiglath-pileser accomplished this feat by overhauling Assyria's imperial policy. He ordered the wholesale deportation of conquered peoples to other parts of the empire. Therefore, when Assyria destroyed Samaria in 722 b.c. (2 Kings 17:1–18), it removed a large percentage of the population to other lands. It also brought other victims of Assyrian expansion into Samaria (Ezra 4:2). Therefore, the Bible places Nineveh's repentance shortly before one of the most remarkable military reversals in world history. Preachers often criticize Jonah for his lack of charity toward the Assyrian people, but it seems he foresaw that an Assyrian revival would bring the downfall of Israel. The book of Isaiah confirms this interpretation: "The Lord will bring upon you and upon your people and upon your father's house such days as have not come since the day that Ephraim departed from Judah—the king of Assyria" (Isa. 7:17). The biblical record of Deuteronomy, 2 Kings, Isaiah, and Jonah agree with what we know about Assyrian history. God raised up the Assyrian Empire as an instrument to fulfill his curse to scatter rebellious Israel.

GREAT POWER TO FORGIVE

Even though God had raised Assyria up to chasten Israel, Assyria went too far in its arrogance and cruelty, as Isaiah 10:5-7, 15 explains:

> Ah, Assyria, the rod of my anger;
>   the staff in their hands is my fury!
> Against a godless nation I send him,
>   and against the people of my wrath I command him,
> to take spoil and seize plunder,
>   and to tread them down like the mire of the streets.
> But he does not so intend,
>   and his heart does not so think;

but it is in his heart to destroy,
and to cut off nations not a few;

. . . .

Shall the axe boast over him who hews with it,
or the saw magnify itself against him who wields it?
As if a rod should wield him who lifts it,
or as if a staff should lift him who is not wood!

It is at this point in biblical history that the prophet Nahum
steps in. God used Assyria to scatter the northern kingdom
of Israel, but Judah looked to the seductive power of Assyria
for salvation rather than to God. Assyria, a mere tool in
God's hand, had exalted itself above God. The Assyrians
mocked the living God. In this context, we find Nahum
saying, "The LORD is slow to anger." God is patient (2 Peter
3:9), but his patience has a limit. Assyria's iniquity is now
complete (cf. Gen. 15:16).

Before God could avenge himself upon Assyria, however, he had to restore his people, who had abandoned
him for Assyrian gods. Nahum 1:3 continues, "The LORD
is . . . great in power, and the LORD will by no means clear
the guilty." In Numbers 14:17, Moses begins his prayer by
pleading, "Please let the power of the Lord be great." Moses
knew that it would require great power for God to forgive
a sin this great. That Nahum 1:3 omits the words "please
let" from this quotation shows that Moses' prayer has now
been answered. Nahum did not ask God to forgive; he
declared the forgiveness accomplished. Even though Judah
had sinned greatly—sinned as grievously as the Israelites
had in Exodus and Numbers—God's great power enabled
him to forgive Judah.

Just as the sins in Exodus and Numbers still carried
grave consequences, Judah's covenant with Assyria resulted
in poverty, destruction, and death. Sennacherib, king of
Assyria from 705 to 681 B.C., boasted that he had "laid
siege to 46 of [Hezekiah's] strong cities, walled forts and

to the countless small villages in their vicinity. . . . I drove out (of them) 200,150 people, young and old, male and female, horses, mules, donkeys, camels, big and small cattle beyond counting."[4] All sin has consequences. With good reason, Solomon declared that "the fear of the LORD is the beginning of knowledge" (Prov. 1:7). Sin is a power (Rom. 7:8). It is foolish to disregard God's commands. It is foolish not to fear the consequences of sin. When we sin, we invite spiritual darkness into our souls. We need God to forgive us, and we also need him to break the power of sin in our lives. This requires great power. It requires God's power. It requires the work of Christ.

JUDGED WITH GREATER STRICTNESS

Christians often make a grave error in their interpretation of Old Testament history. When we read about Israel's sins, we tend to judge Israel harshly. We are right to see these sins as grievous, because the Bible makes this plain. What we in the church have not rightly considered is that we have sinned even more grievously. The writer of Hebrews makes this precise point:

> For since the message declared by angels proved to be reliable, and every transgression or disobedience received a just retribution, how shall we escape if we neglect such a great salvation? It was declared at first by the Lord, and it was attested to us by those who heard, while God also bore witness by signs and wonders and various miracles and by gifts of the Holy Spirit distributed according to his will. (Heb. 2:2–4)

If Israel risked annihilation for their rebellion in Exodus 32 and Numbers 13, how can we believe that we have angered God less? Israel had a limited Bible, while ours is complete and readily available. Israel had a lesser mediator, "for

Jesus has been counted worthy of more glory than Moses" (Heb. 3:3). Most importantly, Israel had only the promise of a Messiah, and we have a glorious gospel. We need to repent of how we have viewed the Israelites. They sinned greatly against God, but our sin is much greater.

Some may think that the above argument minimizes the work of the gospel, for "if you are led by the Spirit, you are not under the law" (Gal. 5:18). I have not minimized the gospel or the extent of Jesus' atonement. Rather, I have sought to demonstrate from Scripture that those of us who have received the full Bible, who have Jesus as a mediator, and who have known the gospel commit a much more serious sin than the Israelites when we love the world more than God. Does the television fascinate you more than the Bible? Do you care more about success at work than God's glory? Do you willingly suffer shame and scorn for the sake of Christ? Ask yourself hard questions, and be willing to answer honestly. Is there anything in your life that excites your passion more than Jesus? If so, you need to consider that the sins listed in the Old Testament are specks, while yours is a log.

If we commit sins more offensive to God than Israel did, we need a more effective mediator than Moses. Moses' intercession stayed God's wrath. Jesus' intercession appeased his wrath. As God stated to Moses, as Moses repeated to God, and as Nahum says to us, "The LORD will by no means clear the guilty." God does not and cannot just look past sin. If your brother is the chief of police and you get pulled over for speeding, you likely will not get a ticket. God, however, "shows no partiality" (Rom. 2:11). Every sin must be paid for. Through the gospel, the one who intercedes for us has also purchased the answer to his prayer. "If we confess our sins, he is faithful and just to forgive us our sins and to cleanse us from all unrighteousness" (1 John 1:9). Notice that the verse says God "is faithful and just," not "faithful and merciful." On the cross, Jesus paid fully for the sins of his bride. The Father now has a legal obligation to Christ to pardon the sin of those whom Jesus redeemed. As John so eloquently says, justice mandates the pardon. Though God will not "clear the guilty," he will accept a substitute. Jesus, the perfect sacrifice, fully drank the cup of God's wrath so that his sheep may be saved.

The Bible wants us to know, believe, and respond to this grace. Grace is freely extended to the worst of sinners. Jesus has paid the penalty for our sin, and God desires that we would repent of our sin and cling to Christ, trusting that his atoning work brings salvation. We must realize, though, that the Bible also wants us to acknowledge our sin—to know how deeply we have offended a holy God. The Bible does not allow us to use grace as a license for sin. We have no right to judge the sins of Old Testament Israel and then to presume upon God's grace to cover our own love for the gods of our culture. Without facing the evil of our own actions, we cannot truly understand the grace offered to us in the New Testament. In the time of Nahum, Judah had sinned grievously but received mercy through intercession. Today we have sinned grievously and have the offer of a full pardon if we will confess our sin and submit to Christ as Lord (Rom. 10:9). Only by seeing just how deeply we have sinned against a holy and righteous God will we comprehend the magnitude of what Jesus did. To be forgiven much is to love much; to be forgiven little is to love little (Luke 7:47). "How shall we escape if we neglect such a great salvation?" (Heb. 2:3).

FOR FURTHER REFLECTION

1. Choose a Bible story in which God restored someone after grievous sin. Find the passage and meditate on it. What were the steps of this restoration?
2. Read Hebrews 7:23–28. How does Jesus' intercession compare to Moses' intercession in Exodus 32 and Numbers 14?

3. Have you judged the Old Testament Israelites for their failures to trust God without recognizing the same sins in yourself? If so, ask God for the ability to see your own sin more clearly, so that you may understand his grace more fully.

4. Jude 4 mentions ungodly men "who pervert the grace of our God into sensuality." What are some ways in which you have presumed upon God's grace and turned it into a license to sin? Will you confess this now, asking God to remove this sin from your life?

CHAPTER THREE

GOD COMES TO EARTH (1:3b–8)

*"Behold, the virgin shall conceive and bear a son,
and they shall call his name Immanuel"*

(which means, God with us). (Matt. 1:23)

After his resurrection, Jesus taught his followers how to interpret the Old Testament. To the two who walked with him on the road to Emmaus, Jesus said, "O foolish ones, and slow of heart to believe all that the prophets have spoken! Was it not necessary that the Christ should suffer these things and enter into his glory?" (Luke 24:25–26). After this rebuke, Luke records that "beginning with Moses and all the Prophets, he interpreted to them in all the Scriptures the things concerning himself" (v. 27). Later Jesus told all the disciples, "These are my words that I spoke to you while I was still with you, that everything written about me in the Law of Moses and the Prophets and the Psalms must be fulfilled" (v. 44). Then, Jesus

> opened their minds to understand the Scriptures, and said to them, "Thus it is written, that the Christ should suffer and on the third day rise from the dead, and that repentance and forgiveness of sins should

be proclaimed in his name to all nations, beginning from Jerusalem." (Luke 24:45–47)

Jesus had discovered God's path for him by reading the Old Testament. He used the forty days before his ascension to teach his disciples to read the Old Testament this way as well.

In order to get a deeper appreciation for Jesus' study of the Old Testament, we go to an event earlier in his life. The Bible gives us only one story about Jesus' life after his early childhood and before his baptism. At the age of twelve, we find Jesus "in the temple, sitting among the teachers, listening to them and asking them questions" (Luke 2:46). This child, who was the Word (John 1:1), had an insatiable desire to learn the Word. Jesus came to understand who he was and what he was to do through studying the Scriptures. Though he was "very God of very God," he "was made man."[1] In his humanity, Jesus studied the Scriptures to know God's purpose for his life.

As the first man who had ever truly fulfilled Psalm 1:2, Jesus' "delight [was] in the law of the LORD, and on his law he [meditated] day and night." All who had gone before Jesus had encountered Scripture with defective and sinful eyes, ears, and hearts. It constantly amazed Jesus that those who had studied the law did not understand what he understood. We hear Jesus ask religious leaders such things as "Are you the teacher of Israel and yet you do not understand these things?" (John 3:10) and "Have you never read what David did, when he was in need and was hungry?" (Mark 2:25). Only a sinless man, fully submitted to God, could humble himself and read the Old Testament as it was meant to be read, rather than twisting it into what he wanted it to say. Jesus did not reinterpret the Old Testament; he interpreted it according to its intended meaning. He wrestled with God to understand Scripture and was rewarded with a deeper understanding of the Bible than anyone had ever had before.

Jesus' fascination with Scripture included Nahum. Though the church has historically neglected this little book, Jesus would not have disregarded it. As Jesus digested Nahum's words, the book contributed to his understanding of his mission. Our task is to consider what makes Nahum unique: how did it add to Jesus' understanding of God's plan for him, and how does it illumine what Jesus did for us?

The prophet Nahum spoke of the Christ 640 years before the incarnation. Two thousand years after Jesus came, we stand guilty of not recognizing the gospel pronouncement made by Nahum, who was among those who preached that "the Christ should suffer and on the third day rise from the dead, and that repentance and forgiveness of sins should be proclaimed in his name to all nations, beginning from Jerusalem." As we search Nahum in order to find the gospel story, we do not reinterpret it; we walk in the footsteps of the greatest mind that the world has ever witnessed. We read Nahum according to the principle that he gave us. All of the Old Testament preaches Christ. To read it in any other way is to read against God's desire and its intended meaning. Each section of Nahum gives unique insights into Jesus' life. As we examine the text before us now (Nah. 1:3b–8), we will see prophecies of Jesus' incarnation, death, and descent into hell.

THEOPHANY

Nahum 1:3b–8 describes a theophany: the manifestation of God on earth. Nahum explains the power of God by explaining the worldly events that would accompany his incarnation. As God would come to earth to accomplish his work, creation itself would strain under the weight of his glory.

Let me pause here to tell you about an experience I once had in a post office. I like books, and when I know I might have to wait, I take a book. Therefore, one day I found myself in a post office line with a box in one hand

and Jonathan Edwards's *Religious Affections* in the other. As I stood in line, I came across these words:

> I know of no reason, why a being affected with a view of God's glory should not cause the body to faint, as well as being affected with a view of Solomon's glory. And no such rule has as yet been produced from the Scripture; none has ever been found in all the late controversies which have been about things of this nature. There is a great power in spiritual affections: we read of the power which worketh in Christians, and of the Spirit of God being in them as the Spirit of power, and of the effectual working of His power in them, Eph. iii. 7, 20; 2 Tim. i. 7. But man's nature is weak: flesh and blood are represented in Scripture as exceeding weak; and particularly with respect to its unfitness for great spiritual and heavenly operations and exercises.[2]

These words struck me deeply. I had been raised Presbyterian, gone to a Presbyterian seminary, and worked in Presbyterian churches. I knew that Edwards profoundly shaped American Presbyterianism. Many consider him the greatest theologian that America has ever produced. I had also been taught that bodily manifestations in worship were suspect. In less than a paragraph, Edwards logically destroyed that suspicion. The convergence of God's glory and human frailty results in physical undoing.

Nahum 1 makes it clear that God's glory also results in creation's undoing. When the Holy God manifests himself on the earth, the mountains, oceans, and forests faint as well. Creation reacts to events throughout Scripture. In Leviticus, humanity's sin horrifies it. As a result, the earth vomits (Lev. 18:28; 20:22). Similarly, Paul wrote,

> For the creation waits with eager longing for the revealing of the sons of God. For the creation was

subjected to futility, not willingly, but because of him who subjected it, in hope that the creation itself will be set free from its bondage to corruption and obtain the freedom of the glory of the children of God. For we know that the whole creation has been groaning together in the pains of childbirth until now. (Rom. 8:19–22)

Creation suffers under the burden of human sin. In response to certain abominations, creation vomits. But when God visits his creation, it trembles and worships.

The book of Isaiah begins with an assertion that farm animals have a greater knowledge of their master than Israel does: "Children have I reared and brought up, but they have rebelled against me. The ox knows its owner, and the donkey its master's crib, but Israel does not know, my people do not understand" (Isa. 1:2b–3). Later on, Isaiah prophesies that the natural world will join in worship: "The mountains and the hills before you shall break forth into singing, and all the trees of the field shall clap their hands" (Isa. 55:12). Jesus even declares that stones have the capacity to worship (Luke 19:40). All of creation surpasses humanity in its ability to hate sin and acknowledge God. When humans are oblivious to spiritual profundities, nature reacts. Nahum 1:3b–8 describes this reaction.

STORM CLOUDS

The theophany begins with "whirlwind and storm." Long before this, whirlwind and storm preceded God's coming in another book.

Keep listening to the thunder of his voice
and the rumbling that comes from his mouth.
Under the whole heaven he lets it go,
and his lightning to the corners of the earth.

After it his voice roars;
he thunders with his majestic voice,
and he does not restrain the lightnings when his
voice is heard. (Job 37:2–4)

This storm preceded Job's receiving of what he had been longing for throughout the book—God's presence. In an utterly humbling experience, "the LORD answered Job out of the whirlwind" (Job 38:1). In this answer, God proclaims his own glory and Job's frailty by examining creation for four chapters. In Nahum, weather again displays God's glory and human weakness. God comes once again in the whirlwind and the storm, but not to converse with a blameless man. This time whirlwind and storm precede God's vengeance against those who have seduced his adulterous bride.

The clause "the clouds are the dust of his feet" (Nah. 1:3) has particular relevance in this book pertaining to Assyria. The Assyrian military caused dread and fear wherever it appeared. A city's first sign of danger came from the dust of thousands of feet—human and horse—rising into the sky as terror approached. Nahum marks God's coming with a much more magnificent dust cloud. The Assyrian army's tool of terror now comes against them on a cosmic scale.

DELIVERANCE AND JUDGMENT

The military image of dust clouds leads into the next images, which recall two of God's greatest military interventions in Israel's history: Egypt and Canaan. God "rebukes the sea and makes it dry; he dries up all the rivers" (Nah. 1:4). God dried up the Red Sea as the culminating event of the exodus, bringing deliverance and judgment. Israel found freedom from bondage by walking between walls of water. Egypt received a final demonstration of God's justice as Egyptian soldiers drowned. God dried up the Jordan River as a precursor to Israel's conquest of Canaan. Again, this action brought deliverance and judgment. God delivered Israel into its own land. He had promised to "come down to deliver them out of the hand of the Egyptians and to bring them up out of that land to a good and broad land, a land flowing with milk and honey" (Ex. 3:8). In Exodus and Joshua, God's dramatic sovereignty over water brought life and death, freedom and destruction. Nahum prophesies that God will use water in this way again (Nah. 2:6, 8).

Nahum's words indicate that God will now intervene. He comes to deliver his people and to judge accumulated sin. In Nahum, though, God comes alone (cf. Isa. 63:3: "I have trodden the winepress alone, and from the peoples no one was with me," and v. 5: "I looked, but there was no one to help; I was appalled, but there was no one to uphold; so my own arm brought me salvation, and my wrath upheld me"). Nahum gives us no Moses and no Joshua. Only God works deliverance in this book. Afflicted Judah plays no part. God alone brings salvation. Deliverance from bondage and the destruction of evil will not come by means of Israel.

CREATION WORSHIPS

My children go to a local Christian school. My wife and I have greatly appreciated the teachers and the staff, who have worked diligently for little pay or recognition. Many of them sacrifice themselves for the sake of our children. I did cringe one day, however, when my son's teacher explained that "the fear of the LORD" (Prov. 1:7) does not really mean fear, but rather reverence. My son received an earful from me about that interpretation. The Bible repeatedly commands us to fear God. For instance, "Fear God and keep his commandments, for this is the whole duty of man. For God will bring every deed into judgment, with every secret thing, whether good or evil" (Eccl. 12:13–14). It tells us, "It is a fearful thing to fall into the hands of the living God" (Heb. 10:31). The Bible calls us to be people who "tremble" at God's Word (Isa. 66:5).

Nahum 1:5 shows that creation obeys God's command to tremble before him. The verse echoes a previous prophecy of the Messiah's coming:

> The voice of one crying in the wilderness:
> "Prepare the way of the Lord,
>   make his paths straight.
> Every valley shall be filled,
>   and every mountain and hill shall be made low,
> and the crooked shall become straight,
>   and the rough places shall become level ways,
> and all flesh shall see the salvation of God." (Luke
>   3:4–6)

Luke quotes Isaiah's prophecy (Isa. 40:3–5) that highways would prepare the way for God's Messiah. Like Nahum, Isaiah declared that the hills would melt when God came down. These words found partial fulfillment as Roman engineers built roads that Jesus would walk. But the hills melt because they know something that our dull hearts do not.

I used to be a youth minister in Delaware. Twice a year a local Christian school would ask me to preach at their chapel. This painful experience involved standing before four hundred mostly bored and lethargic seventh- through twelfth-grade students first thing Tuesday morning. Chapel began with singing. The school had put a handful of students in charge of music. Few besides these appointees opened their mouths. Then I would talk. On one occasion, I preached from Isaiah 6—not "Here I am! Send me" (v. 8), but "Make the heart of this people dull, and their ears heavy, and blind their eyes; lest they see with their eyes, and hear with their ears, and understand with their hearts, and turn and be healed" (v. 10). I explained—to their considerable surprise—that their deadness was the result of God's judgment upon them. Because they did not honor

God, God had made them callous to the only things in this life that truly matter.

Jim Elliot, the martyred missionary, described this phenomenon more eloquently than I can. He wrote,

> You wonder why people choose fields away from the States when young people at home are drifting because no one wants to take time to listen to their problems. I'll tell you why I left. Because those Stateside young people have every opportunity to study, hear, and understand the Word of God in their own language, and these Indians have no opportunity whatsoever. . . . Those whimpering Stateside young people will wake up on the Day of Judgment condemned to worse fates than these demon-fearing Indians, because having a Bible, they were bored with it—while these never heard of such a thing as writing.[3]

Unfortunately, we know that this judgment extends beyond middle and high school. It is not just the children who need entertainment. The angels must watch us in horror. We find athletes running with balls to be utterly consuming, but not the Bible. We are obsessed with—and addicted to—little electronic devices, but not the Bible. We spend hours imbibing wisdom from television, Internet, newspapers, magazines, radio, and podcasts, but not the Bible.

The problem does not stem from Scripture or from God. Nothing is more beautiful, fulfilling, or fascinating than God. The problem is inside us. Our minds are dead to his beauty—or at least dulled and darkened. This cannot be fixed by pandering to the carnal desire of humanity. If our unchurched neighbors find God and Scripture boring, we should not reinvent church to get them in the door. If we in the church find God and Scripture boring, we should not reinvent church to keep ourselves inside the doors. We dare not continue watering down the milk that American evangelicalism increasingly offers. This will only exacerbate the problem. Isaiah 6:10, which I quoted to those four hundred bored students, offers the solution: "Turn and be healed." The Hebrew word translated "turn" is one of the most common in the Old Testament. First-year Hebrew students will find it on a vocabulary quiz within their first weeks of class. It also means "repent."

Isaiah 6:10 is fulfilled right before our eyes. All around us, hearts are dull, ears are heavy, and eyes are blind. We must admit that this includes us. It is the judgment of God, on our form of Christianity, that our buildings are full of people putting in their time who would rather be doing any number of other things. The only cure for this condition is repentance. The mountains recognize God and quake. The hills recognize God and melt. The trees recognize God and clap. The stones recognize God and cry out. We do not recognize God, and we do not react. If we do not repent, creation will stand up against us at the judgment, for it worshiped and trembled while we yawned.

THE CRUCIFIXION

Isaiah prophesied that the mountains and hills would be leveled to prepare for Christ's birth, and the Bible also says that they quaked at his death: "Jesus cried out again with a loud voice and yielded up his spirit. And behold, the curtain of the temple was torn in two, from top to bottom. And the earth shook, and the rocks were split" (Matt. 27:50–51). Creation knew that its master had just died. It shook, trembled, and mourned in horror. For three hours, darkness came "over the whole land . . . while the sun's light failed" (Luke 23:44–45). The creation spoke so clearly during these hours that the Roman soldiers acknowledged that Jesus "was the Son of God" (Matt. 27:54), and the crowds that had mocked Jesus "returned home beating their breasts" (Luke 23:48). The people knew that Jesus was innocent; they knew he was "a teacher come from God" (John 3:2). Despite this, they hardened their hearts.

Even though humanity had hardened its heart toward God and crucified his Son, God did not leave us in this state. He sent his Spirit, his apostle, and his Word to break this hardness. Peter preached that creation had fulfilled the words of the prophets (Acts 2:14–38). Though Joel prophesied these events most clearly, we see them also in a few verses of Nahum (1:3b–5). God came down to deliver his people. The creation recognized this. The mountains quaked, the earth heaved, and the inhabitants beat their breasts. God used the voice of nature, the word of the prophets, the work of his Spirit, and the rebuke of the apostle to "cut to the heart" three thousand people (Acts 2:37, 41). Today, we likewise must heed the voice of creation, which "goes out through all the earth" (Ps. 19:4). We likewise must pray for the Spirit. We likewise must attend to the words of the prophets and apostles. We likewise must turn so that God can heal us.

REFUGE AND WRATH

In the midst of jealousy, vengeance, anger, power, judgment, and devastation, Nahum 1:7 asserts God's goodness. The verse does this because God shelters those who seek refuge in him. We find God protecting his people throughout Scripture. In some cases, the Bible states that God responds because of the righteousness of the person. For example, "The eyes of the LORD are toward the righteous and his ears toward their cry" (Ps. 34:15). This is not the case in Nahum. Nowhere does Nahum suggest that God's intervention comes because of the righteous suffering of his people. Rather, God intervenes in Nahum despite his people's adultery. In the gospel according to Nahum, we are saved not because we are righteous but because we take refuge in God.

In Revelation 2–3, Jesus dictated seven letters. In these letters, Jesus commended and rebuked seven churches. In two cases, Jesus had nothing critical to say of the church. In one case, Jesus had no compliments. To Smyrna, Christ says, "I know your tribulation and your poverty" (Rev. 2:9). To Philadelphia, Christ says, "I know that you have but little power" (Rev. 3:8). It is the Laodiceans who do not realize that they "are wretched, pitiable, poor, blind, and naked" (Rev. 3:17). The two churches that know their weakness and frailty receive praise and protection from Jesus. The church that does not know its poverty receives rebuke, discipline, and an ultimatum. As in Isaiah 6, the only cure—the only possible solution—is humility and repentance.

Nahum's audience had no works to boast in. They had deserted their God, broken his covenant, and sworn allegiance to foreign gods and kings. They no longer had any claim to God's protection. His deliverance in Nahum comes purely by grace, to an afflicted but undeserving people. As we stand on the other side of the cross from Nahum's original hearers, the same offer comes to us. We need protection—not from Assyria, Rome, or any physical enemy, but from God.

Nahum asks in 1:6, "Who can stand before his indignation?" We cannot. Nahum then asks, "Who can endure the heat of his anger?" Certainly not us. Then comes the statement, "His wrath is poured out like fire." Therefore, when verse 7 offers that God will be a stronghold to those who take refuge in him, we must conclude that we need refuge from God himself. The Westminster Confession of Faith confirms this interpretation: "Every sin, both original and actual, being a transgression of the righteous law of God, and contrary thereunto, doth, in its own nature, bring guilt upon the sinner, whereby he is bound over to the wrath of God" (WCF 6.6). We need deliverance—not from the evil outside us, but from the evil inside us. "For out of the heart come evil thoughts, murder, adultery, sexual immorality, theft, false witness, slander. These are what defile a person"

40

(Matt. 15:19–20). We need to be saved from our sin and saved from the one who will execute vengeance because of that sin. At the cross we have refuge, not because of our righteousness, but because of Christ's righteousness. At the cross we have refuge, not because God does not act in wrath, but because God fulfilled Nahum 1:6 by pouring out his wrath upon his own Son. We stand guilty before a holy and righteous judge. We have "unclean lips, and [we] dwell in the midst of a people of unclean lips" (Isa. 6:5). We have sinned grievously against God, and we live among people who have sinned grievously against God. We have no hope apart from God's mercy given to us because of his Son's work. The cross alone can provide us shelter from God. That God would willingly shelter us from his wrath by pouring it out on his Son demonstrates his goodness.

HE DESCENDED INTO HELL

The next verse contrasts God's mercy to the humble with his attitude toward the haughty. Whereas those who sought refuge in God would find him a fortress, those who hardened themselves against God would find him a relentless foe. Notable in this verse is God's promise to "pursue his enemies into darkness." This statement prophesies the physical darkness at the crucifixion, but also Jesus' descent into hell. English versions of the Bible mask this because of a difficulty with the first part of verse 8, which the ESV translates, "But with an overflowing flood he will make a complete end of the adversaries." The last word is problematic. The natural translation of the Hebrew would be "of her place." Different English versions translate the phrase in all manner of ways since it is not obvious who "her" refers to. As we will see later, Nahum makes liberal use of confusing pronouns. In the case of 1:8, "her place" makes sense as an allusion to Ishtar—the patron goddess of Nineveh.

One of Assyria's most important myths, "The Descent of Ishtar to the Underworld," tells the story of how Ishtar managed to travel to the underworld to retrieve her lover, Dummuzi. In Mesopotamian religion, the deities could not travel between the land of the living and the land of the dead. Some deities ruled the underworld; others remained on earth or in heaven. The goddess Ishtar, however, achieved the rare feat of transcending realms.

Nahum links the judgments of destruction and pursuit. In Hebrew poetry, the second line commonly intensifies the first line. Accordingly, verse 8 promises that God will first completely destroy "her place" with a flood. Then he will pursue his enemies into darkness. The second judgment relates to and increases the first judgment.

God may have used a flood to destroy Ishtar's city. Ancient records provide conflicting accounts of this, but it seems that an unusual event caused the Tigris River to breach a wall during the siege of Nineveh in 612 B.C. Explanations range from a natural and timely flood to a feat of military engineering genius. Various records confirm that water caused a portion of the wall to collapse.[4]

After destroying her place, God continues to pursue his enemies into darkness. In both the Bible and Mesopotamian religion, going into darkness suggests the land of the dead. For instance, Job lamented,

> If I hope for Sheol as my house,
>   if I make my bed in darkness,
> if I say to the pit, "You are my father,"
>   and to the worm, "My mother," or "My sister,"
> where then is my hope?
>   Who will see my hope?
> Will it go down to the bars of Sheol?
>   Shall we descend together into the dust? (Job
>   17:13–16)

Likewise, Jesus used "darkness" as a synonym for hell:

> I tell you, many will come from east and west and recline at table with Abraham, Isaac, and Jacob in the kingdom of heaven, while the sons of the kingdom will be thrown into the outer darkness. In that place there will be weeping and gnashing of teeth. (Matt. 8:11–12)

Mesopotamian underworld myths also describe it as a place of darkness. The most famous example of this comes from *The Epic of Gilgamesh*, which describes the underworld as "the house where those who stay are deprived of light. . . . And they see no light, and they dwell in darkness."[5] God will not rest after he has destroyed Ishtar's fortress. This goddess of love and war seduced and ravished God's people. Nahum promises that God will go to any length to hunt down his rivals and punish them.

While an allusion to Ishtar here makes sense, Nahum 1:8 prophesies much more. Remember that Jesus learned about his mission from reading Scripture. He knew that "just as Jonah was three days and three nights in the belly of the great fish, so will the Son of Man be three days and three nights in the heart of the earth" (Matt. 12:40). If Jesus knew that he would descend into the earth, he would have understood Nahum's prophecy of pursuing enemies into darkness to apply to him as well. Jesus would go into utter darkness. His Father and his God would forsake him. He would descend into hell. Jesus would go into the land of death to pursue death itself,

> For he must reign until he has put all his enemies under his feet. The last enemy to be destroyed is death. (1 Cor. 15:25–26)

Because Jesus descended into hell, Paul could declare,

> "O death, where is your victory?
>   O death, where is your sting?"

The sting of death is sin, and the power of sin is the law. But thanks be to God, who gives us the victory through our Lord Jesus Christ. (1 Cor. 15:55–57)

Jesus went into darkness to destroy spiritual powers. He experienced the defilement of sin on the cross by taking the horrors of countless sins upon him for our sakes. In so doing, he broke sin's power over his people. He went into hell and was raised to break the power of death. While Nahum prophesied God's destruction of Ishtar, the book of Nahum ultimately points to Jesus' destruction of Satan's power. The book of Nahum uses ambiguity to apply its message both to historical Assyria and to spiritual powers. The book has much to say to us today who still live and suffer under the influence of "the prince of the power of the air, the spirit that is now at work in the sons of disobedience" (Eph. 2:2). Jesus' life—from birth to resurrection—consisted of a battle with Satan for the souls of his elect. Nahum prophesied Jesus' relentless pursuit of Satan, his destruction of Satan's power over Jesus' people, and his vengeance against Satan for his crimes. Nahum 1:3b–8 places this battle in the cosmic realms, and it ends with a statement that Christ would go into utter darkness in order to obtain complete victory.

FOR FURTHER REFLECTION

1. Read Isaiah 6. Have you ever been overcome by God's holiness? Have you ever been broken over your sin? The New Testament quotes Isaiah 6:10 five times. Jesus used this verse to explain why he spoke in parables. Pray that God would give you eyes that see, ears that hear, and a heart that understands.
2. Read Psalm 19. Note that the first part of the psalm explains how creation speaks. The second part extols the power of God's written Word. How have

you heard God speak through nature? Our ultimate authority, however, is not God speaking through creation, but God speaking through the Bible. The Westminster Confession of Faith describes this as "the Holy Spirit speaking in the Scripture" (WCF 1.10). Have you experienced God speaking to you in this way?

3. Zephaniah 1:12 says, "At that time I will search Jerusalem with lamps, and I will punish the men who are complacent, those who say in their hearts, 'The LORD will not do good, nor will he do ill.'" Nahum describes God's shelter for the humble and his punishment of the proud. Whether or not we fear God depends on whether we believe that he will intervene in the world. Do you live with the knowledge that God will reward and punish?

4. Read Revelation 12. This chapter describes a cosmic battle over the birth of Christ. The chapter ends by saying, "Then the dragon became furious with the woman and went off to make war on the rest of her offspring, on those who keep the commandments of God and hold to the testimony of Jesus" (Rev. 12:17). Do you live with the knowledge that Satan wages constant war against the saints?

CHAPTER FOUR

NAHUM AND PSALM 9
(1:2-8)

*Your word is a lamp to my feet
and a light to my path. (Ps. 119:105)*

I knew that I wanted to be a preacher when I was fourteen. After graduating from college, I went straight to seminary in order to get my ministerial credentials. In seminary, I had to take homiletics: the study of preaching. In this class, we were encouraged to develop sermons with one theme divided into three memorable points and to alliterate them if possible. I confess I never did this well. In fact, only the compulsion of an assignment ever caused me to have three sermon points beginning with the letter *p*.

I have to admit, however, that my professor had a biblical basis for the use of memory aids. Nahum uses a number of these tools—including alliteration. For example, Nahum starts 2:10 with three words that begin with a "Bu" sound (the NRSV attempts to maintain the alliteration by translating these words "Devastation, desolation, and destruction!"). Nahum uses other memory aids as well. He makes liberal use of repetition and assonance. Repetition appears in such verses as 1:2, 2:10, 3:3, and 3:15–16. Assonance refers to "the repetition of identical or similar vowel sounds in the stressed syllables . . . of neighbouring

47

words."[1] Nahum's assonance does not come through in English, but it may be found throughout the Hebrew text.[2] The prophecy begins with a fourth memory aid: an acrostic. In an acrostic, the letters that begin adjacent lines of poetry either proceed through the alphabet or spell a word. All the acrostics in the Old Testament follow alphabetical order. Complete alphabetical acrostics may be found in the Psalms, Proverbs, and Lamentations.

Psalm 119 provides the best example of an Old Testament acrostic. The psalm contains twenty-two sections of eight verses each. In each section, the first letter of each verse begins with the same letter. The initial letter changes from one section to the next, following the order of the Hebrew alphabet. Many English translations mark this by noting the Hebrew letter that starts the lines of each section (you may want to pause here and see this in your Bible). Almost every verse of the psalm mentions God's Word, using synonyms such as "law," "statutes," and "precepts." The acrostic structure emphasizes completeness; it praises God's Word, as the saying goes, from A to Z.

In contrast, Nahum begins with a deficient acrostic. Because of this, the acrostic evaded detection until the late nineteenth century. Then Franz Delitzsch briefly mentioned it while commenting on Psalm 9.[3] The acrostic escaped notice for this long because it only covers half the alphabet, lacks one letter completely, and has four other letters that are not the first letter of the line.

You may wonder how such a structure qualifies as an acrostic. If so, you are in good company. Many have argued that no acrostic exists. The most persuasive—and humorous—voice against an acrostic belongs to Michael Floyd:

In W. H. Auden's "Lay Your Sleeping Head, My Love," much the same phenomenon is evident in lines 8–9, 11–12, 13–14, and 35–36, but no one would seriously suggest that this poem is therefore a latent partial alphabetical acrostic. The initial letters of lines 21–27

48

also happen to spell out *c-o-l-a* and *t-e-a*, but no one would seriously suppose that Auden has therefore made part of the poem from an acrostic based on a list of beverages. Or would they?[4]

According to many scholars, mere chance explains the semi-alphabetic progression of Nahum 1:2–8. The question of whether or not an acrostic exists in Nahum 1 matters, though. Many have used Nahum's broken acrostic as evidence that the Bible we have has deteriorated over the years. The question of why a broken acrostic exists in Nahum relates directly to God's preservation of Scripture. Also, even though Nahum has historically suffered from neglect, the question of an acrostic in it has received more attention than any other issue in the study of the book. For these two reasons, we will spend the rest of this chapter examining this issue.

ACROSTIC THEORIES

Many scholars believe that the acrostic originally existed in a more complete form and that the text has suffered damage. Other scholars dismiss the idea of an acrostic altogether. Some hypothesize that Nahum began his book by adapting an existing hymn of praise to God, but in doing so he took liberties with the acrostic structure of the original hymn. Finally, some have suggested that Nahum had a general purpose for the broken acrostic: he meant to use alphabetic disorder to convey disruption caused by God's coming.

Whichever theory one chooses depends heavily on one's assumptions about the Bible. Those who believe that the Bible contains errors will find the corruption theory a satisfactory explanation. Those who believe that the Holy Spirit has protected the text will reject this explanation. Many who believe that the Bible does not contain error have embraced the coincidence theory. Those who take this view agree with those who hold the corruption view on one point—that Nahum did not intend a broken acrostic. I think Nahum did intend it.

The broken structure makes purposeful allusions to other Old Testament texts. Nahum used the acrostic and anti-acrostic elements to make subtle theological points. Unfortunately, a thorough treatment of this would require a detailed look at these verses in Hebrew, which goes beyond the scope of this book. We can, however, consider the general aspects of this theory.

A WORD ABOUT SCHOLARSHIP

Often scholars will arrive at something of a consensus. This consensus, however, always involves interpreting data on the basis of shared assumptions. The expressions "scholars say," or "scholars believe," or "scholars have discovered" often intimidate those who are not scholars. These expressions convey the idea that smart people have proved something. Behind the expression "scholars have discovered," though, are assumptions about what is logical, reasonable, and likely. Brilliant scholars may have an encyclopedic knowledge of ancient languages and cultures, but basic assumptions about whether God exists, superintends history, and will judge the wicked shape their interpretation of data. It is my hope that this chapter will show that Scripture can be trusted. If we humble ourselves before the Bible, the Holy Spirit will show us the grandeur of the Bible; those who go to Scripture in pride will find it flawed, for God has "hidden these things from the wise and understanding and revealed them to little children" (Matt. 11:25).

Before looking at the text, we need to discuss two points that undermine the corruption theory. First, no ancient textual evidence suggests that Nahum is corrupt. Mainstream scholars used to propose radical changes in order to reconstruct a full acrostic. This changed when the Dead Sea Scrolls were discovered in 1946. These scrolls date to well before the birth of Christ and predate any other existing Hebrew manuscripts by hundreds of years. These scrolls confirmed that scribes had reliably transmitted the Old Testament over the ages. The Nahum Dead Sea texts showed remarkable consistency in transmission. These scrolls forced mainstream scholarship to abandon theories requiring radical reconstruction. Any scholars holding to the idea that Nahum has suffered significant corruption must hypothesize that it happened in the few hundred years between the times of Nahum and the Dead Sea scribes.

Second, scholars have always believed that Nahum was a brilliant poet. While many scholars find the content of Nahum objectionable, all of them recognize literary brilliance in the poetry. One commentator explains, "Nahum, according to these interpreters, is a violent, nationalistic book, one morally repugnant to modern persons. Its moral inferiority, however, does not mask its literary artistry. Nahum is a bad book written well."[5] The best example of this comes from J. M. P. Smith's century-old commentary. Smith's combination of eloquence and disdain for Nahum's message makes him the favorite source of quotes about Nahum's doctrine. Almost all commentaries on Nahum include a colorful quote from Smith about what a bad book it is. Despite this, even Smith admits that Nahum

> has an unexcelled capacity to bring a situation vividly before the mind's eye. His constructive imagination lays hold of the central elements of a scene and with realistic imagery and picturesque phraseology recreates it for his readers. Accurate and detailed observation assists in giving his pictures verisimilitude. . . . Through the whole scene there moves a mighty passion and a great joy which lift the narrative out of the commonplace into the majestic and make of it great literature.[6]

How can scholars universally praise Nahum's brilliant literary skill and still hold that the text is mutilated and patched? Could mutilated poetry still be brilliant poetry? Scholars have suggested emendations not just to Nahum 1:2–8 but to every verse in this prophecy. These conjectures have no basis in the ancient manuscripts. They merely come from an effort to make this prophecy conform to the logic of modern scholars. We agree that the book has been accurately transmitted for the last 2,100 years. We agree that the original author was a literary genius. We should not then turn around and assume that the text must be corrupt because it doesn't conform to what we expect it to say.

We must therefore consider the possibility that this brilliant poet intended the broken acrostic structure. We must be humble enough to consider that ancient writers had a deeper understanding of their own language than we do, who are so far removed in time and culture. We must acknowledge that Nahum knew the Scriptures more minutely than we do. We must recognize that the Bible has a literary complexity worthy of the Word of God.

AN ALLUSION TO PSALM 9

The difficulties in the Bible expose our own limitations. On essential matters of salvation, the Bible speaks clearly. In other places, we have to wrestle. The acrostic features in Nahum present us with a puzzle. I believe that such puzzles were meant to show us beauty and depth in God and his Scripture. I caution you against accepting confident statements about deficiencies in the Bible. There is much we do not understand and much still to be discovered.

There are different explanations for the presence of the acrostic features. I would now like to offer mine. I believe that Nahum framed 1:2–8 to mirror the structure of—and therefore allude to—Psalm 9. Psalm 9 and Nahum 1:2–8 share five structural similarities. First, Psalm 9 and Nahum 1 both contain an acrostic of half of the Hebrew alphabet. Each acrostic begins with the first letter of the Hebrew alphabet, *aleph*. If your Bible puts the Hebrew letters in Psalm 119, this will be the letter over verse 1. The acrostics of Psalm 9 and Nahum 1 both end with the Hebrew letter *kaph* (see Psalm 119:81). These are the only two half-acrostics in the Bible. Second, both acrostics lack one letter. In both cases, the Hebrew letter *daleth* (see Psalm 119:25) is missing. Third, the acrostics in Psalm 9 and Nahum 1 both begin after a title verse that is not part of the acrostic. Fourth, both acrostics have an irregular progression through the letters of the alphabet. Most of the other acrostics in the Old Testament change letters at set intervals of lines, ranging from one line to eight. In both Nahum 1 and Psalm 9, however, the number of lines between letter changes varies. Fifth, both acrostics seem to end prematurely. Despite completing only half the alphabet, the acrostics in Psalm 9 and Nahum 1 end before the section does.

The similarities between the acrostics in Psalm 9 and Nahum 1 are known. A number of scholars have mentioned this in passing. The reason they do not believe that Nahum alludes to Psalm 9 is that mainstream biblical scholarship has also accepted the view that Psalm 9 is textually corrupt. That view actually has a measure of ancient textual support, but this evidence comes from Greek texts rather than Hebrew ones. In the years prior to Christ's birth, ancient scribes translated the Old Testament into Greek. We call this translation the Septuagint. This word comes from the Latin word for "seventy," since legend has it that 70 (or 72) scribes independently translated the Hebrew Scriptures and their translations turned out to be identical. The Septuagint combines Psalms 9 and 10 into one psalm. While it is impossible to know for sure why the scribes believed that the psalms belonged together, it is likely that they did so because Psalm 9 contains an acrostic with the letters from the first half of the Hebrew alphabet and Psalm 10 contains a partial acrostic using some of the letters from the second half. For this and other reasons, scholars today widely hold that Psalms 9 and 10 were originally one psalm.[7]

To further illustrate and expound on this point, it is worth quoting Robert Alter. He has written extensively about the Hebrew Scriptures. Many times he has defended the accuracy of the Hebrew text. However, in *The Book of Psalms: A Translation with Commentary*, he writes that Psalm 9 and 10 are corrupt.

> At some early moment in the long history of transmission, a single authoritative copy was damaged (by decay, moisture, fire, or whatever). Lines of verse may have been patched into the text from other sources in an attempt to fill in lacunae. Quite a few phrases or lines were simply transcribed in the mangled form or perhaps poorly reconstructed. When the chapter divisions of the Bible were introduced in the late Middle Ages, the editors, struggling with this imperfect text, no longer realized that it was an acrostic and broke it into two separate psalms. The result of the whole process, alas, is that we are left with a rather imperfect notion of what some of the text means.[8]

From Alter's perspective, there is little we can rely on in the texts of Psalms 9 and 10.

Do you see how modern assumptions control this reasoning? Nahum 1:2–8 is corrupt because the acrostic is not complete. Psalms 9 and 10 are corrupt because they are divided and their acrostic is also deficient. We start with an idea of what the Bible should be and then declare that the text is corrupt because it does not match our expectations. But why should an ancient Hebrew text conform to modern logic? We should not want it to. This betrays our modern bigotry and arrogance. We are not smarter than ancient writers were. We do not write better. We certainly do not know their literature as well as they did. We do have the benefit of millennia of discoveries and technology that they did not have, but this does not make us better poets than they were. It certainly does not give us cause to dismiss an ancient poetic text because it does not conform to our logic. Our goal is to approach Nahum 1:2–8 with reverence and humility. Much more than giving Nahum the benefit of the doubt, we submit to it as the inerrant Word of God—given to us as God intended.

DAVID'S PRAYER

Nahum's prophecy announces God's intervention. God now comes down to deliver his afflicted people from crushing spiritual and physical adversaries. Nahum uses the broken acrostic structure to show that David's prayer from Psalm 9 is now answered.

Psalm 9:3 thanks and praises God because "when my enemies turn back, they stumble and perish before your presence." There are quite a few thematic similarities between Nahum and Psalm 9. We will initially focus on Psalm 9:5–6:

> You have rebuked the nations; you have made the
> wicked perish;
> you have blotted out their name forever and ever.
> The enemy came to an end in everlasting ruins;
> their cities you rooted out;
> the very memory of them has perished.

These verses bear a strong similarity to Nahum 1:14 ("No more shall your name be perpetuated") and find specific fulfillment in the downfall of Nineveh. A combined force of Medes and Babylonians destroyed Nineveh in 612 B.C. An Assyrian remnant fled the city, but by 605 the Assyrian Empire had been completely blotted out. From 745 to 627, Assyria ruled with absolute control over the greatest empire the world had ever seen. The great buildings of Egypt, Babylon, Greece, and Rome remain. Many of their greatest cities still exist. Not so with Assyria. The destruction of Assyria was so complete that until Austen Henry Layard discovered the buried remains of Nineveh in 1845, much of the world considered the Bible's accounts of Assyrian greatness to be exaggerated. Before then, the location of what had been the greatest city in the world was a mystery. God did indeed root out their cities so that the memory of them faded.

In verse 13, the psalm turns to petition. It cries out for deliverance:

> Be gracious to me, O LORD!
> See my affliction from those who hate me,
> O you who lift me up from the gates of death,
> that I may recount all your praises,
> that in the gates of the daughter of Zion
> I may rejoice in your salvation. (Ps. 9:13–14)

David declares that evil nations have caused their own destruction: "The nations have sunk in the pit that they made; in the net that they hid, their own foot has been caught" (v. 15). He says that God has already "executed judgment" (v. 16). In a verse that points to Nahum's underworld themes, David says, "The wicked shall return to Sheol, all the nations that forget God" (v. 17). Then David cries out to God to intervene: "Arise, O LORD! Let not man prevail; let the nations be judged before you!" (v. 19). The acrostic portion of Nahum 1 answers these prayers precisely. God arises to judge Assyria. He comes down to earth in love and wrath. He comes to deliver his beloved, afflicted people, and he comes to wipe from the earth the kingdom that seduced them. David concludes by saying, "Put them in fear, O LORD! Let the nations know that they are but men!" (v. 20). The Assyrian Empire boasted in its power. The king of Assyria claimed, "By the strength of my hand I have done it" (Isa. 10:13). Now, in Nahum,

God humbles Assyria and shows them that they are at his mercy. Nahum uses his acrostic to allude to Psalm 9 and declare that David's prayer would now be fulfilled. As we look back in history, we see that God did indeed watch over his word to fulfill it (Jer. 1:12).

Pain, suffering, and death exist in this world because our first parents sinned against God. That sin began with a question. Satan possessed one of God's creatures and used it to ask Eve, "Did God actually say . . . ?" (Gen. 3:1). The most important strategy in Satan's war against God, his Christ, and us is to undermine our confidence in God's word. He does this by means of worldly wisdom. The wisdom of the age will always conflict with Scripture. The early church struggled with the conflict between Scripture and Greek philosophy. Some early church fathers sought to harmonize the two, while others did not. The leading thinkers in any age will always have intimidating arguments about why only a fool would believe Scripture. Today, the Harvard professors and Nobel Prize winners tell us that the universe is 13.7 billion years old, that humans evolved from animals, and that emotions are merely chemical reactions. To deny these views makes one appear simple in the eyes of the world. The Bible does not give us a choice, however. "Let no one deceive himself. If anyone among you thinks that he is wise in this age, let him become a fool that he may become wise" (1 Cor. 3:18). To follow Christ requires believing portions of God's Word that make the world scoff. The particular part of Scripture that scoffers find worthy of ridicule changes with the age, but every culture has its scoffers. As you encounter arguments that suggest that Scripture is defective, do not be impressed by the credentials of the scoffer. God asks us to choose an ultimate authority. It can be Scripture. It can be the appointed wise men and women of the age. It cannot be both. Unless we decide that we will trust Scripture regardless of Satan's attempts to undermine it, we will not benefit from it. God hides his truth from the proud and the scoffer. He gives the jewels of his wisdom to those who become fools in the eyes of the world, humble themselves before God, and ask him for wisdom.

FOR FURTHER REFLECTION

1. Read Genesis 3. Notice how Satan sought to undermine Eve's confidence in God's word. Also notice how God does not intervene to defend his word. How does Satan attack our confidence in Scripture today?
2. Read 1 Corinthians 1:17–31. Paul contrasts the wisdom of the world and the wisdom of God. In what areas do you consider the Bible to be deficient compared to current wisdom? If you answered that you do not, perhaps you should think about the question longer. Are there portions of Scripture that you have harmonized or explained away in order not to be offensive to the wisdom of the modern age?
3. The Westminster Confession of Faith explains the reasons to place our confidence in Scripture.

> We may be moved and induced by the testimony of the Church to an high and reverent esteem of the Holy Scripture. And the heavenliness of the matter, the efficacy of the doctrine, the majesty of the style, the consent of all the parts, the scope of the whole (which is, to give all glory to God), the full discovery it makes of the only way of man's salvation, the many other incomparable excellencies, and the entire perfection thereof, are arguments whereby it doth abundantly evidence itself to be the Word of God: yet notwithstanding, our full persuasion and assurance of the infallible truth and divine authority thereof, is from the inward work of the Holy Spirit bearing

witness by and with the Word in our hearts.
(WCF 1.5)

Examine the difference between the various reasons given in the first part of this paragraph for
why we may have confidence with the ultimate
reason that ends the section. We discussed some
of these reasons in this chapter. Why does a true
understanding of Scripture require a work of God in
a person's heart? Why would an unbelieving world
reject Scripture as errant and fallible?

CHAPTER FIVE

DISARMED (1:9–12a)

He disarmed the rulers and authorities and put them to
open shame, by triumphing over them in him.
(Col. 2:15)

My seventh-grade English class not only gave me my first taste of poetry, but also was my first experience with Shakespeare. In that class we read *Richard III*, in what would turn out to be the first of my many academic encounters with the Bard's plays. My Shakespeare books always included a brief introduction to the characters at the beginning of the book, and I often found myself turning there to remind myself of who was who.

From chapter 1:9 onward, reading Nahum could be compared to reading a Shakespeare play that has had the helpful notes, first two acts, scene introductions, and notations identifying the characters removed. After the introductory verse (1:1) and a hymn of praise to God (1:2–8), verse 9 abruptly shifts to a dizzying passage (1:9–15) in which the prophet accuses, condemns, and passes sentence on various adversaries of God without naming any of them.

One could attribute this confusion to textual corruption, literary incompetence, or poetic device. Again, I argue for the latter. Nahum intended the ambiguity. He invited us into a courtroom. We walk in late, though, just as the defendants hear their sentence. We do not know who these defendants are, and it is not clear what they have done. Once again, we need to recognize the poetic nature of this book. Other prophets speak more plainly. They name the characters, spell out the offenses, and proclaim the judgment. Nahum condenses this process into a few words. The characters receive no introduction or identification beyond number and gender. Nahum and God speak to these characters, but who is being addressed changes rapidly and abruptly. The difficulty of the section is compounded for an English reader, since the English language provides no way to distinguish gender and number when the prophet addresses "you."

Before we delve into the significance of these abrupt shifts, it would help to familiarize ourselves with the meager biographical information provided in these verses. Therefore, I have inserted the gender and number of the pronouns when they are not obvious in English. Nahum 1:9–15 reads,

> What do you [masculine plural] plot against the LORD?
>   He will make a complete end;
>   trouble will not rise up a second time.
> For they [masculine] are like entangled thorns,
>   like drunkards as they [masculine] drink;
>   they [masculine] are consumed like stubble fully
>   dried.
> From you [feminine singular] came one [masculine
>   singular]
>   who plotted evil against the LORD,
>   a worthless counselor.
>
> Thus says the LORD,
> "Though they [masculine] are at full strength and many,
>   they [masculine] will be cut down and pass away.
> Though I have afflicted you [feminine singular],
>   I will afflict you [feminine singular] no more.
> And now I will break his yoke from off you [feminine
>   singular]
>   and will burst your [feminine singular] bonds apart."

The LORD has given commandment about you [masculine singular]:
"No more shall your [masculine singular] name
be perpetuated;
from the house of your [masculine singular] gods I
will cut off
the carved image and the metal image.
I will make your [masculine singular] grave, for you
[masculine singular] are vile."

Behold, upon the mountains, the feet of him
who brings good news,
who publishes peace!
Keep your [feminine singular] feasts, O Judah;
fulfill your [feminine singular] vows,
for never again shall the worthless pass through you
[feminine singular];
he is utterly cut off.

We have some detective work to do. Four defendants come
under God's judgment: (1) a group of males, (2) a single
female, (3) a worthless counselor, and (4) a single male.
Nahum did eliminate one mystery in 1:15 by identifying
the woman in 1:12–13 as Judah.

PLURAL MALES

Nahum 1:9 contains three terse statements aimed at a
group of male adversaries:

What do you plot against the LORD?
He will make a complete end;
trouble will not rise up a second time.

To make sense of these words requires attention to both
Scripture and history. The events of Nahum pertain to

a drama that began long before the prophet lived. This minor prophet writes one section of a much larger story. Thanks to archaeologists and linguists, we have access to extensive Assyrian records. By combining knowledge of Assyrian imperialism with careful attention to Nahum's biblical allusions, we can make sense of these three clauses.

Each of the above three statements refers to past Assyrian actions against Israel. Assyria's ascendancy came at God's behest. God raised it up for his purposes, but it did not grasp this. Instead, it glorified itself. Since Assyria served God as a vassal, he would judge Assyria according to its own standards for vassal loyalty.

WHAT DO YOU PLOT?

Assyrian kings subdued nations through superior military prowess. Assyria had no equal for a century, including the years when Nahum lived. Any nation it conquered took a loyalty oath to the king. There was no choice besides agreeing to treaties with crushing conditions. As years passed, nations withered under the demands for exorbitant tribute. These demands included gold, silver, grain, animals, raw materials, and military service. Assyrian subjects longed to be free from this tyranny. Sometimes this resulted in rebellious alliances. When word of these alliances reached Nineveh, however, Assyria acted decisively. Assyrian annals contain numerous notations that a subject king had "plotted" and "devised evil." For instance, Ashurbanipal's annals record, "Azuru, king of Ashdod, plotted in his heart to withhold (his) tribute and sent (messages) of hostility to the kings round about him. Because of the evil he had done, I put an end to his rule over the people of his land."[1] In a more vivid recounting, Sennacherib boasted, "I tore out the tongues of those whose slanderous mouths had uttered blasphemies against my god Ashur and had plotted against me, his god-fearing prince; I defeated them (completely)."[2] One such "plot" resulted in Israel's destruction.

> Against him came up Shalmaneser king of Assyria. And Hoshea became his vassal and paid him tribute. But the king of Assyria found treachery in Hoshea, for he had sent messengers to So, king of Egypt, and offered no tribute to the king of Assyria, as he had done year by year. Therefore the king of Assyria shut him up and bound him in prison. Then the king of Assyria invaded all the land and came to Samaria, and for three years he besieged it.
>
> In the ninth year of Hoshea, the king of Assyria captured Samaria, and he carried the Israelites away to Assyria and placed them in Halah, and on the Habor, the river of Gozan, and in the cities of the Medes. (2 Kings 17:3-6)

Assyria had no tolerance for Israel's scheming. God would have no more tolerance for Assyria's plots "against the LORD." The Assyrians accepted God's blessing—the expansion of their empire, wealth, and fame—but they refused to acknowledge the true cause of their success or give God his portion.

Jesus told a parable that describes the foolishness and consequences of disregarding one's debt to God.

> "There was a master of a house who planted a vineyard and put a fence around it and dug a winepress in it and built a tower and leased it to tenants, and went into another country. When the season for fruit drew near, he sent his servants to the tenants to get his fruit. And the tenants took his servants and beat one, killed another, and stoned another. Again he sent other servants, more than the first. And they did the same to them. Finally he sent his son to

them, saying, 'They will respect my son.' But when the tenants saw the son, they said to themselves, 'This is the heir. Come, let us kill him and have his inheritance.' And they took him and threw him out of the vineyard and killed him. When therefore the owner of the vineyard comes, what will he do to those tenants?" They said to him, "He will put those wretches to a miserable death and let out the vineyard to other tenants who will give him the fruits in their seasons." (Matt. 21:33–41)

Jesus' parables provide simple stories that make the point seem obvious—but as we condemn those in the story, we condemn ourselves.

Everything that we have comes from God. "Every good gift and every perfect gift is from above, coming down from the Father of lights" (James 1:17). Consider just three examples of how God has prepared our vineyard. First, he created the universe and put us on a planet with abundant light, heat, water, and energy. Second, God knit together the roughly fifty trillion cells in each of our bodies. He implanted the information that they need and superintends their incredibly complex processes. Third, we probably have more material resources than 99 percent of all humans who have ever lived. The list could go on and on. Like the tenants in the parable, we must do the work that God has given us to do. We must realize, however, that the work that God gives us to do is infinitesimal when compared to what he has done. Also, let us not forget that even the ability to perform our tasks depends on God's grace.

God has provided for us bountifully. He expects thanks and praise in return. Our human hearts, though, hate to share credit. Like the Assyrians, we delude ourselves by thinking, "By the strength of my hand I have done it" (Isa. 10:13). God patiently gave the Assyrians time to repent. One hundred and thirty-three years would pass from the time when God exalted Assyria to perform his task to the time when he obliterated the empire. During those years, Assyria committed unspeakable atrocities and blasphemies, yet God waited. "The Lord is not slow to fulfill his promise as some count slowness, but is patient toward you, not wishing that any should perish, but that all should reach repentance" (2 Peter 3:9). God waits for you as well. He knows the extent of your cosmic plagiarism. He knows how little you acknowledge his work and grace in your life. He waits. Turn now from all pride. Humble yourself before God. Acknowledge that he has given you everything you have. Acknowledge that you cannot keep yourself alive for one moment, apart from his grace. Give him thanks for all he has done.

A COMPLETE END

Like the first clause of Nahum 1:9, the second clause dictates that the Assyrians will receive the same treatment as they have given others. Jesus explained this system of justice in the Sermon on the Mount.

> Judge not, that you be not judged. For with the judgment you pronounce you will be judged, and with the measure you use it will be measured to you. (Matt. 7:1–2)

While postmodern society uses these verses as a defense against criticism, in reality they should terrify us. Our fleshly nature always looks for fault, and therefore blame, in others. God watches and uses our standard for others against us.

The Assyrians made "a complete end" (Nah. 1:9) of any vassal that plotted against them. The most gruesome example of this occurred when Ashurbanipal destroyed Elam in 639 B.C. Here is the Assyrian scholar Daniel Luckenbill's translation of Ashurbanipal's account:

The sanctuaries of Elam I destroyed totally (*lit.*, to non-existence). Its gods (and) goddesses I scattered (*lit.*, counted) to the wind(s). Their secret groves, into which no stranger (ever) penetrates, whose borders he never (over)steps—into these my soldiers entered, saw their mysteries, and set them on fire. The sepulchers of their earlier and later kings, who did not fear Assur and Ishtar, my lords, (and who) had plagued the kings, my fathers, I destroyed, I devastated, I exposed to the sun. Their bones (members) I carried off to Assyria. I laid restlessness upon their shades. I deprived them of food-offerings and libations of water.

For a (distance) of a month of twenty-five days' journey I devastated the provinces of Elam. Salt and *silhu* (some prickly plant) I scattered over them.[3]

Assyrian pride desired vengeance reminiscent of Lamech's taunt, "I have killed a man for wounding me, a young man for striking me. If Cain's revenge is sevenfold, then Lamech's is seventy-sevenfold" (Gen. 4:23–24). Because of this hubris, Assyria made "a complete end" of the ten northern tribes.

TROUBLE

The Assyrians made a "complete end" of rebels for three reasons. First, their pride demanded vengeance. Second, they wanted to send a message to other vassals that rebellion against Assyria had terrible consequences. The third reason explains Nahum's third clause of 1:9. If a vassal proved rebellious, Assyria destroyed its ability to "rise up a second time." A total devastation of a land would remove all the rebellious elements. The land would never trouble Assyria again.

Through Nahum, God held Assyria to its own standard. As Assyria claimed the right to execute total vengeance upon a vassal who plotted against it, God would execute total vengeance against Assyria for breaking its treaty obligations to him.

Therefore, Matthew 7:1-2 should cow rather than embolden us. No one exercises tolerance. We are all legalists. We all have absolute standards for others' behavior. When they offend these rules, we judge them severely. Only the gospel can liberate us from this legalism. It does this by the fear of God. The same author who recorded Jesus' words, "Judge not, that you be not judged," also wrote,

And in anger his master delivered him to the jailers, until he should pay all his debt. So also my heavenly Father will do to every one of you, if you do not forgive your brother from your heart. (Matt. 18:34-35)

We saw before that the power to show kindness to our enemies comes from God's vengeance. We see here that the ability to forgive comes from God's demand that we forgive others. The fear of the LORD is the beginning of forgiveness.

METHOD OF EXECUTION

While Nahum 1:9 gives the reason for God's judgment, verse 10 explains his method of execution. Whereas the prophet speaks directly to the adversaries in verse 9, he addresses verse 10 to his readers. Nahum says that these men are like "entangled thorns," "drunkards," and "stubble fully dried." Using three similes, he promises their incapacitation. Thorns take over an abandoned area. Drunkards incapacitate themselves. Stubble dries and burns after separation from its root.

Such judgment spans the Bible. The book of Psalms begins with it. The one who loves God's law "is like a tree" (Ps. 1:3); the wicked "are like chaff" (v. 4). Likewise, Jesus said,

I am the vine; you are the branches. Whoever abides in me and I in him, he it is that bears much fruit, for apart from me you can do nothing. If anyone does not abide in me he is thrown away like a branch and withers; and the branches are gathered, thrown into the fire, and burned. (John 15:5–6)

Union with Christ brings nourishment, strength, and fruit. Autonomy results in withering and judgment. Assyria flourished because God raised it up. It refused to thank, praise, or honor God and has now been cut off.

BELIAL

With verse 11, we leave the plural enemies and encounter two new characters. A lone female has sent forth a worthless counselor. This verse allows at least two interpretations—one historical and the other supernatural. In the first interpretation, "you" refers to Nineveh. The Bible often uses feminine imagery to refer to cities. Perhaps the most dramatic instance of this occurs in Lamentations: "How lonely sits the city that was full of people! How like a widow has she become" (Lam. 1:1). According to this interpretation, the worthless counselor was the royal herald. The second possibility is that both parties are demonic. I believe Nahum intended both the historical and the supernatural interpretations.

The events of verse 11 happened when Assyria invaded Judah in 701 B.C. A human messenger went forth from Nineveh to give Jerusalem worthless counsel. This "Rabshakeh" gave much counsel to those quaking behind Jerusalem's walls, and all of it qualified as "evil," "against the LORD," and "worthless."[4] He boasted that no God or king could resist Assyria; should the Jerusalemites choose to trust in God's deliverance, they would "eat their own dung" and "drink their own urine" (2 Kings 18:27). Jerusalem rejected this counsel, Hezekiah humbled himself, and Isaiah prophesied Sennacherib's doom. The Bible considers this event so momentous that three different Old Testament books devote a total of five chapters to telling the story (2 Kings 18–19; 2 Chron. 32; Isa. 36–37). The vileness of Rabshakeh's words also merited mention in Nahum. These insults became a major reason for divine judgment.

Nahum's adjective, "worthless" (appearing in 1:15 also), carries more malice than the English suggests. We could just as easily translate it as the proper name "Belial." Most Hebrew names carry meanings, so it does not surprise us to find such a word here. For instance, Zechariah 3:1 speaks of "Joshua the high priest standing before the angel of the Lord, and Satan standing at his right hand to accuse him." The word *Satan* is a transliteration of the Hebrew word. It means "accuser" or "adversary." Satan's name derives from his actions. Revelation 12:10 calls Satan "the accuser of our brothers." Therefore, one could interpret the figure in Zechariah 3 as "Satan" or "the accuser." If Zechariah used the word as a description rather than as a proper name, we merely have a heavenly attorney bringing charges, not an archangel of evil. This question has caused much controversy, and I believe the New Testament settles the issue: it was Satan accusing Joshua. For our present purposes, however, we only need to note that such words may function as a proper name, a description, or both. In Nahum 1:11 and 15, Nahum definitely used the word as an adjective ("worthless"), but he likely intended the double meaning.

The New Testament confirms that "Belial" is a demonic being. In 2 Corinthians 6, Paul gives this command:

Do not be unequally yoked with unbelievers. For what partnership has righteousness with lawlessness? Or what fellowship has light with darkness? What accord has Christ with Belial? Or what portion does a believer share with an unbeliever? What agreement has the temple of God with idols? (2 Cor. 6:14–16)

The use of *Belial* suggests that Nahum believed that Judah had suffered from a malevolent spirit.

The identification of this messenger as Belial affects our interpretation of the lone female in 1:11. The servant is not greater than the master. As a centurion once said, "I too am a man under authority, with soldiers under me. And I say to one, 'Go,' and he goes, and to another, 'Come,' and he comes, and to my servant, 'Do this,' and he does it" (Matt. 8:9). The one who sends is greater than the one who is sent. If the messenger was demonic, how much more so the master? The goddess Ishtar seems the obvious candidate for an evil feminine power capable of commanding Belial.

THE DATE OF NAHUM

Nahum 1:12 leaves the mistress and her herald in order to address once again the destiny of the group designated by the masculine plural. This time God speaks. The judgment decreed—"they will be cut down and pass away"—confirms our interpretation of 1:9–10. God removes the power that has sustained these men; as a result, they wither.

The first half of verse 12 provides subtle clues that allow us to pinpoint the date of the book. Before examining this, however, we will consider the more obvious ways in which Nahum dates itself. Nahum 3:8–10 compares Nineveh and Thebes and makes it clear that Thebes has fallen. Since the Assyrians conquered Thebes in 663 B.C., we know that Nahum prophesied after this date.

The other chronological landmark occurred in 612 B.C., when a coalition of Medes and Babylonians defeated, plundered, and razed Nineveh. Since Nahum refers to the sack of Thebes in 663 as a past event and the destruction of Nineveh in 612 as a future one, Nahum prophesied during the intervening fifty-one years.

Nahum 1:12 allows us to mark the exact year of Nahum's vision, however. This verse describes Assyria as being "at full strength and many." Therefore, Assyria had not yet started the decline that followed Ashurbanipal's death in 627 B.C.[5] After 627, no Assyrian king proved capable of governing the empire. In just fifteen years, Nineveh would smolder. A few years later, Assyria ceased to exist. Because of this, we may confidently narrow the time period of Nahum's words to 663–627 B.C.

Verse 12 contains another, more subtle clue. The Hebrew word that the ESV translates "at full strength" is the adjectival form of "shalom," the Hebrew word for peace. Astonishingly, Nahum 1:12 says that Assyria is at peace. This time of peace helps us in two ways. First, Ashurbanipal used the word *peace* to announce military victory. For example, he said, "Peacefully I returned to Nineveh, the city of my dominion,"[6] and "With abundant plunder and much spoil in peace I returned to Nineveh."[7] This suggests that Nahum prophesied immediately following a major triumph.

The second aspect of Assyrian "peace" offers a more useful clue. We have already seen that Nahum declared that Assyria would be "cut off." God would incapacitate a nation that no people had been able to withstand. It must have seemed impossible to Nahum's original hearers. American sports fans will use the term *dynasty* for a sports team that wins three or four championships in a short period of time. The Assyrian military had not lost for a hundred years. They had crushed every opponent. But God did cut Assyria off, causing it to wither.

These two events—a major Assyrian victory and the end of Assyrian aggression—happened in the same year. In 639 B.C., Assyria completed a brutal and prolonged subjugation of Elam by sacking the capital city of Susa. Then something remarkable happened in the historical record. It goes blank.

Explaining the astounding nature of this fact requires some background information. Almost all of what we know about Assyria, and much of what we know about ancient Mesopotamia, came from the nineteenth-century excavations of Nineveh. Most of the written records came from a single source—Ashurbanipal's enormous library. Ashurbanipal prided himself in being a scholar.[8] This was no small boast. The Assyrian scribes wrote in Akkadian, using a cuneiform alphabet. Wedge shapes of specific patterns represented sounds. Put together they formed words. Reading and writing this language requires tremendous skill. It took decades of work by some of Europe's brightest scholars to first decipher it. Therefore, when Ashurbanipal claimed to be skilled in scribal arts, he either told an outlandish lie or he had received a rigorous education in his youth. Though he likely exaggerated his ability, we may be certain that he did have a passion for reading, because he managed to accumulate a library of 22,000 cuneiform clay tablets. (The preferred mode of official writing involved preparing a soft clay tablet, marking on it with a stylus, hardening it, and then giving it to the recipient.) Ashurbanipal employed numerous scribes to copy existing texts for his library. He confiscated other tablets by sending officers throughout his realm to relieve libraries of their contents. So when you read *The Epic of Gilgamesh* in tenth grade, you had Ashurbanipal to thank. Even though the story originated many centuries earlier, we would have little of the text without Ashurbanipal's relentless collection, copying, and preservation of Mesopotamian literature. In addition to preserving existing texts, Ashurbanipal's scribes also generated thousands of tablets of their own. These included such disparate genres as pay stubs, incantations, and poetry. Ashurbanipal outdid all other ancient kings in his obsession for keeping written records.

This brings us back to the issue of dating Nahum. Nahum 1:10 and 12 explain two otherwise inexplicable mysteries of Assyrian history. In these two verses, Nahum prophesies that "they" will "be cut down and pass away." This judgment of incapacitation is reiterated throughout the rest of the prophecy. Therefore, we may surmise that Nahum pronounced this judgment in 639 B.C. because that date marked the end of Assyria's military conquests and Ashurbanipal's records. In 639, God incapacitated the Assyrian war machine, and it just withered away in silence. The king whose bloodlust surpassed that of all his warrior predecessors stopped sending out his armies. This king who prided himself in his literary abilities and had preserved the minutest details of his reign no longer wanted his history recorded. For twelve years—from 639 to 627—we know almost nothing about Assyrian history.[9] During this period in Assyrian history, the empire was at peace.

Nahum 1:12 describes these years perfectly. Ashurbanipal had subdued his last rebel. Nations still feared the empire. But God broke the power of Assyria. The Assyrian military became drunk, dry thorns. From 639 to 627, Assyria decayed from the inside, though no one seemed to realize it. With the passing of the dreaded king, Assyria no longer had a name or an army that could subdue its neighbors. Nahum 1:9–12a was fulfilled exactly.

UNION WITH CHRIST

We all too often read Scripture as if it were hyperbole. Some of the statements in the Bible seem so outlandish that we consciously or subconsciously treat them as exaggerations. They were meant to inspire us and move us down the path of righteousness, we think, but surely they were not meant to be taken that seriously. Jesus made such a statement in John 15, when he said, "Apart from me you can do nothing" (15:5). Jesus claims to be the vine by which we receive nourishment. Only by remaining in the vine can we bear fruit that will be of any use. In this passage and others, Jesus uses an agricultural image to teach that God will test us with time. "Every branch in me that does not bear fruit he takes away, and every branch that does bear fruit he prunes, that it may bear more fruit" (John 15:2). This verse confirms that what was true of Assyria will be true of us. God raised them up. He equipped them to fulfill his purpose. They rebelled against him. God suffered their rebellion for a time. He is patient. The time came, though, when the Assyrian kings had tried God's patience too long. He cut them off and they became "like chaff that the wind drives away" (Ps. 1:4). How much more has God raised us up and given us every opportunity to know his will and to call out to him? Jesus spoke no hyperbole. You either know your total dependence on Christ or you walk blindly in this world. God is gracious and patient. He upholds us despite our folly, yet he calls to us to repent of our arrogance. Those who drink deeply from God's Word will grow in strength and height and fruit, as Psalm 1 promises. Those who eschew Scripture for other sources of strength will inevitably find the folly of this choice, though it may come only when the books are opened on the last day (Rev. 20:12). God's patience has a fearsome consequence. When we forsake "the fountain of living waters" for "broken cisterns that can hold no water" (Jer. 2:13), we do not notice our withering. It happens slowly. Should you live your life apart from Christ, you will end up not like a great tree but "like stubble fully dried" (Nah. 1:10). I encourage you now to put this book down, confess any and every way that you have forsaken Christ for this world, and plead with God to unite you—or reunite you—to Christ.

FOR FURTHER REFLECTION

1. Have you ever thought about all the ways in which God sustains you? Have you ever taken time to thank him? Consider making an extensive list of all that he has done and continues to do for you. Work through this list, thanking him for each item.

2. How have you viewed Jesus' command, "Judge not, that you be not judged" (Matt. 7:1)? What are the sins that you judge most harshly? How would

you fare if God used that same standard on you? Often the sins that we hate the most in others are the ones we refuse to see in ourselves. Consider asking a few people who know you well how you have sinned in these areas.

3. Read John 15. In what areas of your life do you know that you must have Christ's strength the most? In what areas do you most depend on your own effort? Are there areas in which you used to depend upon Christ but no longer do? Have you seen your strength or fruitfulness wither in those areas?

CHAPTER SIX

GOOD NEWS (1:12b–15)

*Fear not, for behold, I bring you good news of great joy
that will be for all the people. (Luke 2:10)*

My dad is a developer. These days, he builds assisted-living homes on the East Coast, but he has had a long career building everything from town houses to skyscrapers. When I tell people how many times I moved during my childhood, they often assume that Dad was in the military. When the economy would change locally or nationally, we would move in order for Dad to build something else somewhere else.

Every time we moved, my mom wanted to get my sister and me established—socially and spiritually—as quickly as possible. The last two times we moved, we ended up in Presbyterian churches. In these churches, I was taught the doctrine of election, but I did not embrace it. I found the arguments for predestination unconvincing and continued to reject it through college.

When it came time to choose a seminary, I ended up at Reformed Theological Seminary in Jackson, Mississippi, for reasons other than doctrine. My theological turning point came in a class titled "Genesis to Joshua." In this class, Dr. John Currid argued that the Old Testament tells the story of God's promise in Genesis 3:15 to "put enmity between you and the woman, and between your offspring and her offspring." Dr. Currid interpreted this verse as a prophecy of the battle between Satan and Christ as well as of the conflict between Christ's chosen and the line of Satan. I have always loved the Old Testament—yet in all the arguments about predestination, I had never heard anyone argue for predestination from the Old Testament. As Dr. Currid showed us this doctrine through the pages of the Pentateuch, I found his arguments compelling and convincing.

I must admit, however, that the Bible speaks most clearly about election in Romans 9.

> This means that it is not the children of the flesh who are the children of God, but the children of the promise are counted as offspring. For this is what the promise said: "About this time next year I will return, and Sarah shall have a son." And not only so, but also when Rebekah had conceived children by one man, our forefather Isaac, though they were not yet born and had done nothing either good or bad—in order that God's purpose of election might continue, not because of works but because of him who calls—she was told, "The older will serve the younger." As it is written, "Jacob I loved, but Esau I hated."
>
> What shall we say then? Is there injustice on God's part? By no means! For he says to Moses, "I will have mercy on whom I have mercy, and I will have compassion on whom I have compassion." So then it depends not on human will or exertion, but on God, who has mercy. (Rom. 9:8–16)

The argument in Romans 9 develops from the beginning verses of Malachi; God explains his love to an afflicted Judah by means of his love for Jacob and his hatred for Esau.

When we go back to Genesis and examine the lives of Jacob and Esau, however, we discover something interesting. While God did bless and prosper Jacob, he also afflicted him many times. Jacob did not have an easy life. His difficulties culminated when God wrenched his hip (Gen. 32:24–25). After many years, Jacob looked back on the hardships of his life and called God "the God who has been my shepherd all my life long to this day" (Gen. 48:15). In contrast, the Bible records no such struggles for Esau. Esau had Isaac's love. He had strength and skill. He prospered and became a wealthy warlord (Gen. 33). Esau despised the promises of God, and God granted Esau everything he wanted—power, wealth, food, and wives. Malachi 1 and Romans 9 demonstrate that God shows his love by chastening his elect. Sometimes he shows his hatred by giving reprobate men and women everything that they want.

COMPASSION THROUGH AFFLICTION

This brings us to Nahum 1:12b. Here God says to Judah, "Though I have afflicted you, I will afflict you no more." Nahum 1:12b–15 contains Nahum's message of good news to Judah, and the message starts with affliction.

We must be careful not to restrict this doctrine to Israel and the Old Testament, for Hebrews 12 asks,

Have you forgotten the exhortation that addresses you as sons?

"My son, do not regard lightly the discipline
of the Lord,
nor be weary when reproved by him.
For the Lord disciplines the one he loves,
and chastises every son whom he receives."

It is for discipline that you have to endure. God is treating you as sons. For what son is there whom his father does not discipline? If you are left without discipline, in which all have participated, then you are illegitimate children and not sons. (Heb. 12:5–8)

Similarly, in Jesus' stern words to the church of Laodicea, he says, "Those whom I love, I reprove and discipline" (Rev. 3:19).

Our culture has lost this doctrine. We talk about God's love without paying attention to what the Bible says about it. In many churches, the pastor explicitly teaches that God's love will result in prosperity like Esau had. Few pastors explain how God's chastening of his people demonstrates his love. This failure comes from not recognizing the true horror of sin.

Sin is a power (Rom. 7:17). It dwells inside us and works to destroy everything good. Unfortunately, we all too often hate the effects of our sin much more than the sin itself. I had a friend who went to medical school. At one point, I asked him what kind of medicine he wanted to practice. He answered in the negative by saying he did not want to be an internist. When I asked him why, he explained that internists most often treat sicknesses that are self-inflicted—arising from unhealthy habits. The doctor medicates the symptoms but also tells the patient that his lifestyle must change. The medication is received gratefully—the advice, well, not so much. My friend believed that this would lead to a career of futility: treating symptoms of disease, but not being able to deal with the root cause.

We have a similar—but much more serious—problem with sin. Jesus came, not only to save us from the effects of our sin, but also to save us from our sin. Sin destroys our lives. Every human wants deliverance from the effects of sin, but few humans hate their sin. We do not understand how truly evil and destructive it is. We do not understand how deeply it offends and angers God. Therefore, we go to God like a patient going to an internist. We want to keep our sin and our sinful lifestyle, but we want God to heal the destruction that this sin has caused.

God alone understands the depth of sin's evil. He alone hates it with a pure and perfect hatred. He cannot abide sin in his beloved, and he will go to any length to destroy it. Theologians call this doctrine the perseverance of the saints. The Westminster Confession of Faith explains, "They, whom God hath accepted in His Beloved, effectually called, and sanctified by His Spirit, can neither totally nor finally fall away from the state of grace, but shall certainly persevere therein to the end, and be eternally saved" (17.1). God differentiates between those who are truly his children and those who are not by disciplining those he loves for their ultimate good. One of the best evidences that a person belongs to Christ is that God works to thwart the enjoyment of sin. If God has done this in your life, be grateful and thank him. If, however, your plans have gone well and God has not interfered, Hebrews suggests that you may be "illegitimate children and not sons" (Heb. 12:8), for even Jesus "learned obedience through what he suffered" (Heb. 5:8).

In Nahum 1:12, Judah has received such affliction. Judah left her Lord and committed adultery with Assyria. The prophet Ezekiel would later describe this episode with some of the most explicit language in the Bible.

> Her sister Oholibah [Jerusalem] saw this, and she became more corrupt than her sister [Samaria] in her lust and in her whoring, which was worse than that of her sister. She lusted after the Assyrians, governors and commanders, warriors clothed in full armor, horsemen riding on horses, all of them desirable young men. And I saw that she was defiled; they both took the same way. But she carried her whoring further. She saw men portrayed on the wall, the images of the Chaldeans portrayed in vermilion, wearing belts on their waists, with flowing turbans on their heads, all of them having the appearance of officers, a likeness of Babylonians whose native

land was Chaldea. When she saw them, she lusted after them and sent messengers to them in Chaldea. And the Babylonians came to her into the bed of love, and they defiled her with their whoring lust. And after she was defiled by them, she turned from them in disgust. When she carried on her whoring so openly and flaunted her nakedness, I turned in disgust from her, as I had turned in disgust from her sister. Yet she increased her whoring, remembering the days of her youth, when she played the whore in the land of Egypt and lusted after her paramours there, whose members were like those of donkeys, and whose issue was like that of horses. Thus you longed for the lewdness of your youth, when the Egyptians handled your bosom and pressed your young breasts. (Ezek. 23:11–21)

God allowed Judah to suffer the consequences that came from making an alliance with Assyria.

Assyria had an insatiable desire to conquer. Assyrian armies went forth on campaigns for the sake of the glory of their high god, Asshur. They believed that the whole earth should be under his dominion. Once a nation came under the control of Assyria, their problems had only begun. Assyria demanded crushing tribute from their vassals. Assyria also sought to integrate conquered nations into Assyrian culture. For instance, some of the abominations practiced by King Manasseh likely came from his affiliation with Assyria (see 2 Kings 21; 2 Chron. 33).

The Assyrians were perhaps the most brutal and cruel society in history.[1] The Assyrian annals continually gloat about their evil.

I killed large numbers of his (troops), the bodies of his warriors I cut down like millet(?), filling the mountain valleys (with them). I made their blood run down the ravines and precipices like a river, dyeing plain,

countryside and highlands red like a royal robe(?).
His warriors, the mainstay of his army, bearers of
the bow and lance, I slaughtered about his feet like
lambs, I cut off their heads.[2]

God chose this evil empire to afflict Judah, but now Nahum
declares the Assyrian judgment at an end.

YOKE AND BONDS

In order for God to end the Assyrian affliction, he had to
"break his yoke from off you" (1:13). Nahum here alludes
to Assyrian writings. Over and over again, Assyrian kings
described conquered people as under their yoke. "One of
the most common Assyrian metaphors is the 'yoke' as a
symbol to depict Assyrian suzerainty. The subjugated vassal
is pictured as an ox wearing the 'yoke' of its master, the
Assyrian king. . . . This metaphor is distinctly Assyrian; it
occurs rarely in the literature of other ancient Near Eastern
nations."[3] Assyria claimed, and God agreed, that Judah had
served Assyria as a draft animal.

In Nahum 1:13, God promised to deliver Judah twice, for
Judah had two problems: external and internal. We know
from 1:12 that the root of Judah's affliction came not from
Assyria but from God. The Assyrian armies were merely a
tool in God's hand. He had used that tool to chasten Judah's
adulterous heart. Jesus taught,

> You have heard that it was said, "You shall not com-
> mit adultery." But I say to you that everyone who
> looks at a woman with lustful intent has already com-
> mitted adultery with her in his heart. (Matt. 5:27–28)

Judah's heart brought about the treaty with Assyria. Judah
needed salvation, not only from its outward oppressor, but
much more from its own defiled nature. "Out of the heart

come evil thoughts, murder, adultery, sexual immorality, theft, false witness, slander. These are what defile a person" (Matt. 15:19–20). Jesus came to cleanse our evil hearts. The gospel according to Nahum declares this as well. God uses affliction to make his people hate their sin. By causing us to know the bitterness of our defilement, he causes us to "cry because of [our] taskmasters" (Ex. 3:7).

God's deliverance required more than a snapping of fingers, though. Judah had entered into a spiritually binding covenant with Assyria. We have no archaeological record of the actual covenant that Judah signed, but we have treaties that Assyria made with other nations. We may safely infer that Judah had sworn fealty to Assyrian gods and kings. We also know that this treaty included severe curses should Judah break its oath. An extensive curse section found its way into most ancient Near East treaties. Though the Assyrians lacked creativity in some ways, when it came to composing curses they proved quite adept. I have included a number of direct quotes from Assyrian sources so that you may see the connections with Nahum, but if you are curious about the most brutal Assyrian curses, and if your stomach can take it, look up the Vassal Treaty of Esarhaddon on the Internet.[4] It ends with very thorough curses.

Our modern, materialistic culture does not abide curses. I doubt that any society in the history of the world has had less regard for the spoken word. The ancients were not so naive. All people lie (Num. 23:19), but our ancestors took their oaths and vows more seriously than we do. They believed that oaths held spiritual power. They believed that breaking oaths brought consequences. The Bible holds this view as well. The Westminster Assembly viewed oaths so seriously that the Confession of Faith contains an entire chapter on the subject.

Judah had sworn allegiance and servitude to Assyrian deities. They had agreed to come under horrific penalties should they fail to live up to their oaths. Judah's deliverance required much more than just military victory. Judah had entered into a spiritual marriage. It had to be undone. Isaiah had spoken of such an annulment years before:

> Therefore thus says the Lord God,
> "Behold, I am the one who has laid as a foundation
>   in Zion,
>   a stone, a tested stone,
> a precious cornerstone, of a sure foundation:
>   'Whoever believes will not be in haste.'
> And I will make justice the line,
>   and righteousness the plumb line;
> and hail will sweep away the refuge of lies,
>   and waters will overwhelm the shelter."
> Then your covenant with death will be annulled,
>   and your agreement with Sheol will not stand.
>   (Isa. 28:16–18)

It was a small matter for God to destroy Assyria's military. The deliverance of Judah from evil powers would be a much larger problem.[5]

Our father, Adam, brought all humanity under a curse (Gen. 3:17–19). God curses idolaters and their children (Ex. 20:4–5). The apostle Paul pronounced that "all who rely on works of the law are under a curse" (Gal. 3:10), and he placed a curse on "anyone [who] has no love for the Lord" (1 Cor. 16:22). The words *curse, cursed, curses, cursing,* and *accursed* appear in the English Standard Version of the Bible 208 times. Our eyes tend to glaze over as we read these words, but God takes them seriously. These curses are not merely put aside. They come to pass. Only the blood of Christ can break the curse. Even then, Jesus did not just sweep them away; he became the curse.

> Christ redeemed us from the curse of the law by becoming a curse for us—for it is written, "Cursed is everyone who is hanged on a tree"—so that in Christ Jesus the blessing of Abraham might come to

the Gentiles, so that we might receive the promised
Spirit through faith. (Gal. 3:13–14)

We are familiar with the idea of Christ's substitutionary
atonement. The elect benefit from a legal transaction
whereby their sin transfers to Christ and Christ's righteousness transfers to them. Galatians 3 shows that there is a
similar transfer of curses. We have come under Adam's
curse, Moses' curse, and other curses. Only the substitutionary atonement of Christ can annul them.

YOUR GRAVE

The compassionate words of verse 13 turn into a sentence of doom in verse 14, as the prophecy gives its attention
to the single male adversary. So far in the book, this man
has not spoken. He has not acted. The first reference to him
came a few words earlier, when God promised to "break his
yoke from off" Judah (v. 13). Whatever this man did to earn
this fate, Nahum has not told us. The pronouncement begins,
"The LORD has given commandment about you." The judge
has spoken. The prophets declare God's judgments. Their
words raise up kingdoms and tear them down (Jer. 1:10).

This judgment contains three parts. God will cut off this
man's name, his religion, and his life. This powerful ruler
now stands before God's bar of justice utterly helpless. Every
mention of this man for the rest of the book will reinforce this
judgment. The closest that he comes to acting throughout
the entire dismantlement of his realm is "He remembers
his officers" (Nah. 2:5). The decree of God, pronounced by
a prophet, proves sufficient to erase his line, end Assyrian
religion, and wipe earth's most powerful city from memory.

The meaning of "No more shall your name be perpetuated" (1:14) will have to wait until the identity of this
mystery man is revealed in 3:18. The other two judgments
came quickly and decisively. Assyria shared a common

religion with Babylonia. They had a similar history. They used the same language. They taught the same myths. They worshiped the same deities—with one notable exception. The Assyrians worshiped Asshur as their high god. Polytheistic cultures worshiped a pantheon of gods. Yet each religion had a chief deity. The Assyrians distinguished their god Asshur from the chief gods of other nations in two ways. First, they saw a greater distance between Asshur and the other gods. The enormity of this gulf caused one Assyriologist to write, "The supreme god, Assur, is often spoken of in language which at first sight seems monotheistic."[6] Second, Asshur's character had only one dimension. He was a war-god. "Asshur was, indeed, in later times the spirit of conquering Assyria personalized. We do not find him regarded as anything else than a war-god. We do not find him surrounded by any of the gentler attributes which distinguish nonmilitant deities."[7] My children saw a play today, and one of them commented on the lack of character development. Asshur too lacked character development. He was a god only an Assyrian could love. When Assyria fell, Asshur fell. No other people ever willingly worshiped him, and no conquering people absorbed him into their pantheon, as often happened with other gods. With the demise of Asshur, Assyrian religion ended also. Thus the words "from the house of your gods I will cut off the carved image and the metal image" (1:14) found perfect fulfillment.

The last sentence of 1:14 requires little elaboration here. We have seen before that God's promise to "make your grave" found fulfillment in such a total destruction of Nineveh that its location remained unknown until the mid-nineteenth century.

THE GOOD NEWS

One of the greatest challenges that I faced when I first became a solo pastor was liturgy. I arrived in West Virginia knowing little about the subject, and I landed in a church where the liturgy was a big deal. The church gave me grace, and I learned. We worked our way through questions about "psalms and hymns and spiritual songs" (Eph. 5:19). I looked for songs based in Scripture and relevant to the theme of the service. Since we celebrated communion often, we sang Twila Paris's song "How Beautiful" a number of times. The last stanza of that song reads,

> How beautiful the feet that bring
> The sound of good news and the love of the King
> How beautiful the hands that serve
> The wine and the bread and the sons of the earth.[8]

The title of the song and the first line of this stanza come from Paul's quote in Romans 10:15 of Isaiah 52:7. Isaiah wrote, "How beautiful upon the mountains are the feet of him who brings good news, who publishes peace, who brings good news of happiness, who publishes salvation, who says to Zion, 'Your God reigns'" (Isa. 52:7). Paul placed this quote in the midst of one of the greatest missions passages in the Bible. Nahum 1:15 shows remarkable similarities to Isaiah 52:7 in both words and theme.

In the days before telecommunications, nations relied upon human transportation of messages. Both Isaiah 52:7 and Nahum 1:7 use the image of a messenger running through mountains to deliver a message of liberation. The watchmen on the wall look out (Isa. 52:8), see the feet running, know the content of the message by the manner of the messenger, and "break forth together" (v. 9) into worship.

Now imagine yourself on the wall of a Judean city. Your ancestors sold your nation into slavery to Assyria. You witnessed unspeakable atrocities committed by Assyrian soldiers and even worse blasphemies committed by your own Assyria-loving king. You lived in fear of the next time the chariots would come. Then one day a man comes. He has news: Nineveh is no more. Perhaps those who witnessed Allied forces liberate their nation from the Nazis know how those Judeans felt on that day.

Unfortunately for Judah, the respite would not last long. The chariots did return. Not Assyrian ones, but Babylonian. The same Babylonians who razed Nineveh would march on Jerusalem three times before Nineveh's burial mound turned thirty years old. The third time, Jerusalem's fate would hardly seem better than Nineveh's.

Nahum said, "Never again shall the worthless pass through you; he is utterly cut off" (1:15). If applied to Assyria, this promise came about. No other Assyrian army or herald would come. We must wonder, however, how Judah remembered these words as the horrors that the Rab-shakeh foretold came about through Babylonian weapons.

We may look back at the partial fulfillment in 612 B.C., knowing that the Holy Spirit intended a much greater deliverance than when the prophecy first found expression. The book of Jeremiah tells us that, though God delivered Judah from Assyria, Judah's adulterous heart remained. Though the historical record tells us that Nahum's utterances were correct, Nahum 1:15 prophesies a final deliverance not accomplished in the prophet's lifetime. The words mark the end of such affliction.

This end came by Christ. In one stroke, he conquered sin, death, and Satan. He broke the power of sin, so that he could accomplish Ezekiel's promise of "a new heart, and a new spirit" (Ezek. 36:26). Until this happened, external deliverance had no relevance. He conquered death, so that we need fear it no more. "O death, where is your victory? O death, where is your sting?" (1 Cor. 15:55). It is the third point that Nahum foretold most clearly. Belial (1:15) is broken. The one who seduced our ancestral king into signing over the kingdom has been judged.

Let us look now at the middle portion of Nahum 1:15. In response to the messenger's feet, Nahum commands, "Keep your feasts, O Judah; fulfill your vows." Judean worship had fallen into disrepair. The basic tenets of the Torah had given way to depravity and oppression. What does God free us to do? As Moses had told Pharaoh, "We will go with our young and our old. We will go with our sons and daughters and with our flocks and herds, for we must hold a feast to the LORD" (Ex. 10:9). God delivered the Israelites so that they could worship. God delivered Judah so that it could worship. God does not just free us from oppression. We leave one master for another. We come to him. We worship our deliverer.

The good news of Nahum 1:12–15 "pierc[es] to the division of soul and of spirit, of joints and of marrow, and discern[s] the thoughts and intentions of the heart" (Heb. 4:12). I have tried to wield these verses skillfully, in order to lay bare the intentions of your heart. Do you see the horrendous nature of sin in your life? Do you see the desperate reality of it? We all know seemingly healthy people who went to the doctor and received a dreaded diagnosis of cancer. We have watched them wage a merciless war against these renegade cells by afflicting their bodies with toxic treatments. We have understood their choices, for the evil of the disease merits such drastic measures. We have known some who have died, and others who came through cancer-free. We have mourned the former and shared in the joy of the latter when the final laboratory report came back clear. Only those who understand the deadlier cancer in their soul can love the God who afflicts in Nahum 1:12. Only they may know the true ecstasy of verse 15.

Those years of wrestling with liturgy brought me to a conclusion. How the worship service appears does not matter. Talent, fine instruments, and sophisticated electronics do not please God. Orthodox creeds, finely crafted prayers, and eloquent sermons serve only to blaspheme God when coming from people who honor God with their lips while their hearts are far from him (Isa. 29:13). In such cases, God would rather have "one among you who would shut the doors, that you might not kindle fire on my altar in vain!"

(Mal. 1:10). The one who knows God and knows his or her sin will behave as the cancer patient does. This person will travel anywhere and spend whatever it takes to find the one most capable of cutting, poisoning, and burning out the defilement in the body. The scars will become a badge of honor. The doctor will become a hallowed hero. Similarly, your true love for Christ is revealed by how much you love him for his merciless war against your flesh, so that you may unite with him "without spot or blemish" (2 Peter 3:14).

FOR FURTHER REFLECTION

1. Read Hebrews 12. Have you ever considered God's discipline as evidence of his love? Have you ever asked for God's discipline? Why or why not?
2. Read Romans 7. Notice how much Paul hates the sin that lives in him. Notice too how much he desires to be rid of it. How many times have you prayed for God to heal the consequences of your sin? How many times have you begged him to remove the power of sin? Notice that Paul's conclusion is triumphant doxology: even though he is powerless to defeat his sin, he is assured that God will ultimately deliver him "through Jesus Christ"!
3. Read Ezekiel 16. Consider how strongly God hates our defilement. Ask God to give you the ability to see your sin the way he sees it, and so to feel the joy of having its burden lifted from you in the gospel.

CHAPTER SEVEN

THE WEAPONS OF OUR WARFARE (2:1–5)

*For though we walk in the flesh, we are not waging
war according to the flesh. For the weapons of our
warfare are not of the flesh but have divine power to
destroy strongholds. (2 Cor. 10:3–4)*

A s chapter 2 begins, the book of Nahum addresses the reader. Instead of dialogue, intricate word pictures allow us to witness Nineveh's siege. We watch as the city scrambles to prepare its defenses. We see the attack commence. Then—almost instantly—the city falls. What could possibly have brought Nineveh to its knees so quickly? One man could—a "scatterer" (2:1). The greatest military power that the world had ever seen gives way before one of God's servants. How? In this chapter, we seek to answer this question, but not out of mere curiosity. The answer has profound implications for each of us.

NAHUM AND BABEL

Explaining how Nineveh fell to the scatterer begins in ancient history—even from Nahum's perspective. Nahum chose the word *scatterer* intentionally; it links Nineveh's coming judgment to one of the distant past. He meant to take us back to Genesis 10–11. After the flood, Noah's descendants travelled east, settled in Mesopotamia, and began to build cities.

> Cush fathered Nimrod; he was the first on earth to be a mighty man. He was a mighty hunter before the LORD. Therefore it is said, "Like Nimrod a mighty hunter before the LORD." The beginning of his kingdom was Babel, Erech, Accad, and Calneh, in the land of Shinar. From that land he went into Assyria and built Nineveh, Rehoboth-Ir, Calah, and Resen between Nineveh and Calah; that is the great city. (Gen. 10:8–12)

Nineveh was founded in a time of united human rebellion.

When the flood ended, God commissioned Noah to "be fruitful and multiply and fill the earth" (Gen. 9:1). In direct rebellion against this command, Noah's descendants decided to build "a city and a tower with its top in the heavens" (Gen. 11:4). They agreed together, "Let us make a name for ourselves, lest we be dispersed over the face of the whole earth" (Gen. 11:4). Rather than trusting God and obeying his word, these early peoples sought security in numbers and buildings and the reputation that came from both. Nineveh was always a city that lived to make a name for itself by defying God. In Genesis, "the LORD came down" (Gen. 11:5), and he would do so again in Nahum (Nah. 1:2–8). In Genesis, God "dispersed them" (Gen. 11:8). Many centuries later, Nineveh would receive the same treatment. The word "dispersed" (Gen. 11:4, 8) and the name "scatterer" (Nah. 2:1) come from the same Hebrew verb. We are meant to read Nahum 2 through the lens of Babel.

ONE MAN

God begins his assault on the world's greatest and most heavily fortified city with a single man. The irony may be lost on us, but Nahum's audience would have expressed shock, awe, or disbelief that God would send one man against this fortress. In the years since Sennacherib had moved the Assyrian capital to Nineveh, the wealth of the ancient Near East had poured into the city. Assyrian armies had plundered endlessly, and tribute streamed to Nineveh year after year from subjugated foes. Three successive kings—Sennacherib, Esarhaddon, and Ashurbanipal—had used the slaves, money, and material from pillaged nations to expand, embellish, and fortify Nineveh. "Nineveh was an almost impregnable fortress. On the low hills surrounding three sides of the city forts guarded the approaches to the metropolis, while the Tigris flowed by on the west. Beyond its massive walls the city was guarded by a system of moats and canals, and beyond the latter, outworks added further defenses."[1] More importantly, in Nahum's time, Assyria's military needed no walls. No force had withstood them for one hundred years. Who could go against Nineveh and not only survive, but scatter the city?

The New Testament gives us the answer. Jesus came against the nations of the world and established his kingdom. Ironically, the prophet Daniel had explained this to the very man responsible for Nineveh's downfall. One night Nebuchadnezzar had a dream that troubled him. Daniel interpreted the dream and told Nebuchadnezzar that God would destroy the kingdoms of the world and scatter them to the wind. "And in the days of those kings the God of heaven will set up a kingdom that shall never be destroyed, nor shall the kingdom be left to another people. It shall break in pieces all these kingdoms and bring them to an end, and it shall stand forever" (Dan. 2:44). The rock that demolished the kingdoms of the world was Christ.

ROBBING THE STRONG MAN'S HOUSE

Jesus once asked, "How can someone enter a strong man's house and plunder his goods, unless he first binds

the strong man? Then indeed he may plunder his house"
(Matt. 12:29). By beginning the question with the word
how, Jesus indicated that success against the strong man
required using the proper method. In order to plunder the
strong man, one must first incapacitate him.

The New Testament tells the story of Jesus' battle with
Satan. According to Revelation 12, this battle began with
a war in heaven at the time of Christ's birth. Then, at age
thirty, Jesus was led by the Holy Spirit into the wilderness
to confront his ancient enemy. For the first time in history,
a human being completely withstood Satan. Never before
had a human survived the temptations of flesh, glory, and
power without sin. After this, Jesus and his followers began
a systematic dismantling of Satan's kingdom. Evil spirits
shrieked in terror before the Lord's Christ. Even humble
fishermen made Satan's servants flee. The major blow,
however, came at the cross. There Jesus drank the full
cup of God's wrath and entered into hell. But on Sunday
he rose. He conquered death and hell. He had bound the
strong man. Just before Jesus ascended, he told his disciples
that they now had his authority. He sent them into all the
world to continue plundering Satan's fortress. This they
did. In the decades after Jesus' death, the church spread
rapidly. The prophecy of Daniel 2 was coming to pass. A
fortress much more formidable than Nineveh crumbled
before this band.

Today Christ's church has the same charge. We are to
advance against Satan's strongholds, knowing that they
must fall. Unfortunately, many today wonder how this
can be true. In much of the Western world, Christianity
seems in decline. Scholars label Europe as post-Christian.
Moral standards in the United States have changed rapidly
in recent years. Those of us in the West must ask whether
we truly have the power to stand against Satan's kingdom,
let alone destroy it.

The answer to this question still stands: the Bible clearly
says that Christians have the necessary power to make

Satan flee. The problem is not that the Bible is insufficient. The Bible is sufficient. The church in the West has a methodological problem. We want to accomplish Jesus' Great Commission without using his method. Jesus charged his church to take up the cross. We were supposed to endure lives of dishonor before a watching world, sacrificing ourselves for the sake of his glory. As we became weak, God would respond. He would do his work. Through our lives and deaths, those around us who hated God would be confronted with his holiness, their sin, and his grace. The Holy Spirit would bless our work, take our broken lives, and multiply our seed as it fell to the ground and died (John 12:24). Instead, we chose a different path. We would be cool. We would be relevant. We would show the watching world that they could keep their lives as-is and add Jesus to them. Instead of using the methods of the apostles, we adopted worldly marketing techniques and increased the size of our buildings, and the salt lost its saltiness.

Let me put it another way. In Job 41, God describes to Job the strength of Leviathan. He says in verse 8, "Lay your hands on him; remember the battle—you will not do it again!" In the Old Testament, Leviathan carries the double connotation of giant serpent and spiritual enemy (Ps. 74:13–14; Isa. 27:1). Whether in the physical or in the spiritual realm, Job stood no chance against this creature.

Why then do we believe that sound systems, giant TVs, and sports fields will be effective in dismantling Satan's kingdom? How will huge edifices, coffee shops, and entertaining speakers win spiritual victories? "For still our ancient foe doth seek to work us woe; his craft and pow'r are great; and, armed with cruel hate, on earth is not his equal."[2] You may object that none of these things are bad. I ask only that you consider the weapons you use. If you go to confront an enemy who is immeasurably more eloquent, powerful, shrewd, tactical, experienced, and ancient than you, why would you choose buildings and TVs? What are the methods that your church uses to "lay your hands on"

Satan? How are you going to destroy his kingdom? You must choose carefully,

> for though we walk in the flesh, we are not waging war according to the flesh. For the weapons of our warfare are not of the flesh but have divine power to destroy strongholds. (2 Cor. 10:3–4)

If we are honest, we have judged the methods of Christ too costly. We have sought to be Christians and win the world for Christ without living the shameful life that Christ requires. Jesus plainly says, "Whoever does not bear his own cross and come after me cannot be my disciple" (Luke 14:27). We cannot be cool or honored or respectable in the world's eyes if we want to follow Christ. Jesus told his disciples, "I chose you out of the world, therefore the world hates you" (John 15:19).

HUMILITY

I have chosen in this chapter to focus on only one aspect of Nahum 2:1–5: the means by which we may demolish a stronghold. For the sake of brevity, I will examine only five of the means that God has given us for this task: humility, prayer, the Holy Spirit, fasting, and Scripture. We begin with humility because two Bible passages promise that Satan will flee before a humble Christian:

> "God opposes the proud, but gives grace to the humble." Submit yourselves therefore to God. Resist the devil, and he will flee from you. (James 4:6–7)

> Humble yourselves, therefore, under the mighty hand of God so that at the proper time he may exalt you, casting all your anxieties on him, because he cares for you. Be sober-minded; be watchful. Your adversary

100

the devil prowls around like a roaring lion, seeking someone to devour. Resist him, firm in your faith. (1 Peter 5:6–9)

The contrast with Job 41:8 could not be stronger. This terrifying, amazing, ancient being flees before Christians who have humbled themselves before God. Paul tells us that "we do not wrestle against flesh and blood, but against the rulers, against the authorities, against the cosmic powers over this present darkness, against the spiritual forces of evil in the heavenly places" (Eph. 6:12). According to James and Peter, only a humble person stands any chance in such a contest.

Tragically, Christian leaders of all sorts tell us, "Don't pray for humility, you just might get it." Yes, if you pray for humility, God will honor that prayer. Yes, having your pride wrenched from you will be an excruciating experience. Notice the similarity between the words *excruciating* and *crucified*. "I have been crucified with Christ. It is no longer I who live, but Christ who lives in me. And the life I now live in the flesh I live by faith in the Son of God, who loved me and gave himself for me" (Gal. 2:20). God commands this. You must humble yourself; you must crucify your flesh. If you do not humble yourself now, God will do it at the judgment.

> The haughty looks of man shall be brought low,
>   and the lofty pride of men shall be humbled,
> and the LORD alone will be exalted in that day.

> For the LORD of hosts has a day
>   against all that is proud and lofty,
>   against all that is lifted up—and it shall be brought
>   low. (Isa. 2:11–12)

You see, humans are delusional creatures. David asks us, "How long will you love vain words and seek after lies?"

(Ps. 4:2). Our pride comes from insanity. We seek after and embrace lies that tell us that we do not need God, that we can handle life on our own.

Let me pause here for another illustration. As I mentioned before, my father builds assisted-living homes. His firm tries to purchase prime real estate in urban areas. This requires zoning approval from the city council. His projects have often been controversial because some believe that the city should not designate prime real estate for elderly care. I do not wish to discuss the pros and cons of zoning laws, but only to show that we refuse to acknowledge that we will get old and decrepit. We somehow think that frail, elderly people have done something wrong to end up in this condition. Yet the reality is that, unless the Lord returns, most of us will end up like them. "The LORD gave, and the LORD has taken away" (Job 1:21). He gave you a body. He gave you health. He gave you money. He gave you friends, family, and skills. He will take them all away. You cannot keep them. Your looks and talents, your health and wealth—everything that you have came from God. If you take pride in any of those things, you live in a delusion that you somehow deserve them. You did not earn them. They are gifts. To take pride in any of this makes you delusional. You may like your fantasy world more than the one in which you depend upon God's grace for all things. If God is merciful, he will rescue you from the delusion. His judgment would be to leave you in your insanity.

We cannot fight Satan without humility, for without humility we cannot depend upon God. If we do not depend upon God, Satan will not flee. He will laugh, strategize, and destroy us in time. We cannot love God without humility, for only humility will allow us to see how much God has done for us. Paul charges us to "earnestly desire the higher gifts" (1 Cor. 12:31). Surely humility ranks as one of the highest. It also ranks as one of the least desired.

PRAYER

Humility will naturally lead to prayer. Prayer does not depend on discipline or righteousness. It depends on desperation. A humble person knows his or her need of God. A proud person sees prayer as an obligatory Christian duty of little effect. As Jonathan Edwards says, a person's private prayer life reveals the true state of his soul. According to Edwards, a true convert

> sees himself still to be a poor, empty, helpless creature, and that he still stands in great and continual need of God's help. He is sensible that without God he can do nothing. A false conversion makes a man in his own eyes self-sufficient. He saith he is rich, and increased with goods, and hath need of nothing; and knoweth not that he is wretched, and miserable, and poor, and blind, and naked. But after a true conversion, the soul remains sensible of its own impotence and emptiness, as it is in itself, and its sense of it is rather increased than diminished.[3]

Conversion means that God has converted someone. God has changed a proud, hateful heart into one that desires God above all else. Edwards goes on to say that with conversion a person acquires new desires. God becomes the ultimate desire of the heart. Out of longings for things that only God can fill comes a desperation to have God give himself. This person will pray. The self-sufficient person has no need of prayer, apart from the pride of having accomplished the prayer. Do you pray in private? If you do not, Edwards has strong words: "If you have left off calling upon God, it is time for you to leave off hoping and flattering yourselves with an imagination that you are the children of God."[4] If you do not pray, you believe yourself more capable than God is of handling your needs. You also do not primarily desire the things that only God can give. Your heart longs for earthly things, not for the treasures of heaven.

No meaningful spiritual victory comes without perseverance in prayer. Jesus told two parables to drive home this point. In the parable of the persistent widow (Luke 18:1-8) and the parable of the friend at midnight (Luke 11:5-8), Jesus taught that one must struggle in prayer over a period of time to achieve results. If our time, talent, and money can win the world for Christ, we need not pray; we need only recruit more wealthy and talented people. If the world lies in bondage to an evil spiritual power that will yield only to obedient and weak servants of a crucified king, we must pray. One of the most eloquent statements of this came from a man who won spiritual victory after spiritual victory in inland China—one of the spiritually darkest places on earth at the time. Hudson Taylor wrote to an aspiring missionary, "We understand North Honan is to be your field; we, as a mission, have tried for ten years to enter that province from the south, and have only just succeeded. It is one of the most anti-foreign provinces in China. . . . Brother, if you would enter that province, you must go forward on your knees."[5] These spiritual victories demand much from those who would win them. No such victory can be won without persevering in agonizing prayer, asking that God would pour forth his Spirit and break the powers of hell that currently reign. If we are so foolish as to take on "that ancient serpent, who is called the devil and Satan" (Rev. 12:9) without prayer, the consequences will be horrific.

FASTING

Some of John the Baptist's disciples came to Jesus with this question: "Why do we and the Pharisees fast, but your disciples do not fast?" (Matt. 9:14). Jesus responded by saying, "Can the wedding guests mourn as long as the bridegroom is with them? The days will come when the bridegroom is taken away from them, and then they will fast" (Matt. 9:15). Jesus expected that his disciples would fast. The Sermon on the Mount provides another evidence of this. In the middle of the sermon, Jesus talks about the motive for three spiritual activities: giving, praying, and fasting. In each case, Jesus says that our reward will depend upon the heart behind the actions. Those who give, pray, and fast so that others will see their righteousness will receive no further reward. Those who give, pray, and fast out of a desire to please God will receive rewards from God. By including fasting with prayer and giving, Jesus demonstrated that fasting should be part of the normal Christian life.

I bring this up because God has provided fasting as a weapon against Satan. While the Bible makes it clear that fasting done as a religious exercise accomplishes nothing (Isa. 58; Zech. 7:1–7; Matt. 6:16–18), the Bible also teaches that fasting done out of a hunger for God accomplishes its purpose. We see fasting as a precursor to powerful moves of God throughout the Bible. Moses fasted for forty days while he received the Ten Commandments (Deut. 9:9–18). This fast resulted in God's revealing his law to his people and the world. Elijah fasted for forty days when he fled from Jezebel (1 Kings 19:8). When God spoke to him, he gave Elijah instructions for overthrowing Ahab's dynasty and training new prophets in Israel. Ezra fasted in mourning over Israel's sin (Ezra 10:6–17). This fast brought about Israel's repentance regarding intermarriage with pagan peoples. Nehemiah fasted over the condition of Jerusalem (Neh. 1). This fast resulted in the rebuilding of Jerusalem and the repentance of its inhabitants. Esther and the Jews fasted for three days to save the Jewish people (Est. 4:15–17). Daniel undertook two partial fasts (Dan. 1; 10). These fasts resulted in God's imbuing him with the wisdom that would allow him to understand mysteries and to prophesy the coming of Christ. Anna worshiped in the temple "with fasting and prayer night and day" (Luke 2:37). Because of this, God allowed her to see his Christ and to prophesy regarding him. Jesus fasted for forty days before facing Satan in the wilderness (Matt. 4:1–11; Luke 4:1–13). This fast empowered him to overcome Satan and begin his ministry. This partial list shows that God has ordained fasting as a precursor to spiritual power and breakthrough.

I want to consider one last example in more detail, because this one has particular relevance to Nahum and to our situation today. In the days of the early church, the church of Antioch gathered to pray and fast. Note the result:

> Now there were in the church at Antioch prophets and teachers, Barnabas, Simeon who was called Niger, Lucius of Cyrene, Manaen a lifelong friend of Herod the tetrarch, and Saul. While they were worshiping the Lord and fasting, the Holy Spirit said, "Set apart for me Barnabas and Saul for the work to which I have called them." Then after fasting and praying they laid their hands on them and sent them off. (Acts 13:1–3)

We live on the other side of this event. We know the remarkable expansion of the gospel that came through Paul's missionary efforts. We tend to attribute much of this to Paul's natural talents. God, though, waited for the church to fast. Antioch's first fast revealed God's will. The second fast set that will in motion. The Holy Spirit did not allow Jesus to begin his ministry until he had fasted. The Holy Spirit did not allow Paul to begin his ministry without fasting either. The Bible does not give us an equation. Fasting will not guarantee victory. The Bible does teach us to fast. It also gives numerous examples of satanic strongholds that fell after God's people fasted. If you desire to see victory over the satanic power in this world, I encourage you to ask God for the ability and desire to fast.

THE HOLY SPIRIT

The early church faced a daunting task. When Jesus ascended, the church numbered "about 120" (Acts 1:15). Jesus had commissioned them to take the gospel to "all nations" (Matt. 28:19). From the perspective of worldly wisdom, they could have had no expectation of fulfilling this command. The Jewish community in Jerusalem had shouted for Jesus' crucifixion. The Roman world revered Greek philosophy and participated in pagan ritual. Fortunately for us, these first believers did not have the option of relying on reputation, money, and eloquence. Because of this, they had to rely on God's methods. Also, they had clear instructions from Jesus not to take matters into their own hands. Jesus' disciples had spent years walking with and learning from Jesus. They had witnessed and performed miracles. And yet, according to Jesus, they were not equipped for the task ahead of them. Jesus "ordered them not to depart from Jerusalem, but to wait for the promise of the Father, which, he said, 'you heard from me; for John baptized with water, but you will be baptized with the Holy Spirit not many days from now'" (Acts 1:4–5). In reference to these verses, Hudson Taylor once asked, "Since the days before Pentecost, has the whole church ever put aside every other work and waited upon Him for ten days, that [the Spirit's] power might be manifested? . . . We give too much attention to method and machinery and resources, and too little to the source of power."[6] Taylor's words stand today. Rather than realizing that we have no hope apart from the movement of God's Spirit, we often rush into Satan's territory without the power that Jesus prescribed.

It may be argued that since Jesus spoke to his disciples before Pentecost, and since we now live after Pentecost, the need to wait for the Spirit no longer pertains to us. You may be wondering if I am propounding a second baptism of the Spirit. I believe that baptism of the Holy Spirit comes upon a believer at his or her conversion. I do not believe that we need a second blessing. What we do need is to depend upon the Holy Spirit, and that is something that most of us in the Reformed tradition have done a miserable job of. Let me illustrate this in two ways. First, if we met for coffee and I asked you to tell me all that you know about God the Father, how much could you tell me? If I then asked you to tell me about Jesus, how long could you talk? If I then asked you to teach me the doctrine of the Holy Spirit, what would you say? If you are like most people whom I have encountered in Reformed churches, the discussion of the Holy Spirit would not take long. We hold that "there are three persons in the Godhead; the Father, the Son, and the Holy Ghost; and these three are one God, the same in substance, equal in power and glory" (WSC 6). The doctrine that the Father, the Son, and the Holy Spirit are equal in power and glory, however, is not usually reflected in our knowledge of, and dependence upon, the Holy Spirit.

The second illustration comes from Reformed creeds. I have a book titled *Reformed Confessions Harmonized*. It puts seven confessions and catechisms in columns. This enables the reader to look up a specific doctrine and compare what the Belgic Confession, the Heidelberg Catechism, the Second Helvetic Confession, the Canons of Dort, the Westminster Confession, the Westminster Shorter Catechism, and the Westminster Larger Catechism say about it. For instance, if you want to compare their teachings about the Lord's Supper, you turn to pages 220–29 and compare the teachings side by side. The book has forty large pages on the Ten Commandments. If you were to look at the section on the Holy Spirit, you would find one lengthy sentence from the Belgic Confession, one question from the Heidelberg Catechism, and one question from the Westminster Larger Catechism. That's it. Of the two pages that *Reformed Confessions Harmonized* dedicates to the doctrine of the Holy Spirit, the vast majority is white space.[7]

You may think I am not being fair. Each of these seven creeds discusses the Holy Spirit. I agree that they do. But they do not dedicate sections to him. I want to be clear. I believe that these documents provide phenomenal doctrinal teaching and are among the best theological works ever written. I also greatly value their teaching on the Lord's Supper and the Ten Commandments. I do not criticize these sections or question whether they deserve the pages. I also recognize that Reformed theology and Reformed theologians emphasize the necessity of the Holy Spirit's role in salvation in a way that other traditions have not. But while we say that the Holy Spirit is essential to our Christian lives, we often neglect the Spirit in our teaching. This book is not the place to correct this slight. I only wish to bring it to your attention and to encourage you to search the Scriptures regarding the Holy Spirit. Also, I commend Hudson Taylor's words to you again. We need to devote more of our effort to crying out for the Holy Spirit and waiting upon him for the power to do ministry.

SCRIPTURE

When Jesus was tempted in the wilderness, he adopted a remarkable strategy. Satan attacked him with worldly wisdom, but he responded only with Scripture. As in the garden of Eden, Satan argued on the basis of human reason. Jesus knew better than to debate Satan on those grounds. The world judges Scripture to be foolish (1 Cor. 1:18), but God considers the world's wisdom to be foolish (v. 20). If we try to use whatever version of wisdom our culture considers "common sense" at the moment, Satan will darken our minds as he did Eve's. If we hide God's Word in our hearts (Ps. 119:11) and use it against Satan, we will get the victory.

God has given us his Word, and he will hold us accountable for it. In the story of the rich man and Lazarus, the rich man asked for a supernatural visitor to warn his family. Abraham replied, "They have Moses and the Prophets; let them hear them" (Luke 16:29). The rich man believed that his family needed something greater than Scripture to convince them. They would believe the miraculous, he asserted (v. 30). Abraham denied this: "If they do not hear Moses and the Prophets, neither will they be convinced if someone should rise from the dead" (v. 31). According to Jesus, nothing has more power than Scripture. We make a horrendous error if we heed the rich man's suggestion—if we seek to use means other than Scripture to convince people who will not be convinced by Scripture. According to Jesus, this plan has no hope. Only Scripture can change rebellious hearts. What is more, only Scripture will "destroy strongholds" (2 Cor. 10:4). Though humans may disregard Scripture as foolish, Satan does not. Where Satan holds people in bondage, Scripture can break his hold when no worldly means can.

STRENGTH IN WEAKNESS

This chapter has emphasized one point: God will bring incredible victories through his servants if they will use biblical means. Similarly, we have no expectation of biblical fruit from worldly means. "Do not be deceived: God is not mocked, for whatever one sows, that will he also reap" (Gal. 6:7). Our fleshly efforts have no more hope of success than Judean soldiers could have expected against Assyrian armies. I believe that Nahum prophesied about Jesus when he announced the coming "scatterer," but he also foretold the advance of the church. Jesus gave his authority to his followers. Though it does not seem possible, Jesus even promised that "whoever believes in me will also do the works that I do; and greater works than these will he do" (John 14:12).

I encourage you to think back over the five weapons listed above: humility, prayer, fasting, the Holy Spirit, and Scripture. If you found deficiencies in your spiritual knowledge or practice, I would ask you to ask God to supply what is lacking. If you have not yet had the courage to pray for humility, please ask God to give you the courage. If you do not pray out of desperation, please confess your arrogance to God and ask him to show you how needy you really are. If you have never fasted, consider whether you would be willing to try. Fasting is difficult. It may not feel like a breakthrough. It will bring ugly, sinful things to the surface. As it does, ask God to cleanse and heal you. If you do not know much about the Holy Spirit, the Bible gives a tremendous promise to you.

> What father among you, if his son asks for a fish, will instead of a fish give him a serpent; or if he asks for an egg, will give him a scorpion? If you then, who are evil, know how to give good gifts to your children, how much more will the heavenly Father give the Holy Spirit to those who ask him! (Luke 11:11–13)

If you have tended to "lean on your own understanding" (Prov. 3:5), please understand that only Scripture will be effective in spiritual battles. Ask God to give you a mind disciplined enough to "take every thought captive to obey Christ" (2 Cor. 10:5).

We need Christ. We need him at every turn. He has given us an impossible task, but he has equipped us with sufficient tools. "The race is not to the swift, nor the battle to the strong" (Eccl. 9:11). Victory belongs to those who will trust in the means that God has provided. "Some trust in chariots and some in horses, but we trust in the name of the LORD our God" (Ps. 20:7).

FOR FURTHER REFLECTION

1. Find a passage in the Bible where God's people had success against spiritual "strongholds" (2 Cor. 10:4) and meditate on it. What methods did they use?

2. Have you ever been in a situation where you sensed supernatural evil? If so, how did you handle it? Have you ever meditated on the biblical teachings regarding demonic forces? How has this chapter affected your views about your "adversary the devil"?

3. Have you ever fasted? If so, what type of fast did you choose? How long did you fast? Pray and ask God if he would have you fast now. Ask him what you should fast for and what type of fast you should choose. In *A Hunger for God*, John Piper offers an excellent introduction to fasting. If you would prefer a shorter treatment, the chapter on fasting in *Celebration of Discipline*, by Richard Foster, is also helpful.

4. Read John 14–16 and pay attention to the teaching about the Holy Spirit. How much do you know about the Holy Spirit? How does that knowledge affect your daily life?

CHAPTER EIGHT

REVERSAL (2:6–10)

He has shown strength with his arm;
he has scattered the proud in the thoughts of their hearts;
he has brought down the mighty from their thrones
and exalted those of humble estate;
he has filled the hungry with good things,
and the rich he has sent away empty. (Luke 1:51–53)

The Lion, the Witch, and the Wardrobe first appeared in print in 1950, just a few years after Nazi control of Europe had come and gone. England had suffered through air attacks, but was spared the occupation that many other nations had endured. The events of World War II colored C. S. Lewis's work. Indeed, the Pevensie children find themselves in Narnia only because the bombing of London sends them to an old professor's house in the country.

The White Witch's control over Narnia must have reminded Lewis's first readers of Nazi rule. The Witch controlled Narnia through terror. She had no legal claim to rule. Once Aslan appeared in the country, many of the animals defied her openly and civil war broke out. At this point in the book, we find the following interchange:

> "The Queen of Narnia and Empress of the Lone Islands desires a safe conduct to come and speak with you," said the dwarf, "on a matter which is as much to your advantage as to hers."

> "Queen of Narnia, indeed!" said Mr Beaver. "Of all the cheek—"
>
> "Peace, Beaver," said Aslan. "All names will soon be restored to their proper owners. In the meantime we will not dispute about them."[1]

As German tanks rolled over Europe, Nazi officers took over local government and billeted themselves in the homes of the aristocracy. Like the Witch, they took titles that did not belong to them.

Lewis's first readers also witnessed the restoration. Allied armies had rooted out the imposters. Nazi sympathizers who had prospered during the period of German control received harsh treatment at the hands of their countrymen. The German ascendancy had come and gone. Those who had cast their lot with the Germans had enjoyed temporary benefits and then faced long-lasting humiliation.

Of course, Lewis knew this theme first from Scripture. Throughout the Bible, we learn that "the last will be first, and the first last" (Matt. 20:16). The Bible teaches that the world languishes under a usurper more evil than Adolf Hitler or Queen Jadis. It teaches that those who align themselves with "the ruler of this world" (John 12:31; 14:30; 16:11) may receive privileges and honor for a time, but the great reversal will come. Those who have remained loyal to the true king will receive reward and honor. Those who have betrayed him will be destroyed.

Nahum 2:6–10 tells the story of that reversal. Nineveh had set itself up as ruler of the world. It had dominated through terror and lived in luxury. But the true king has now returned, and the proud have fallen.

A PALACE ON THE SAND

Because of the way Nahum intertwined themes throughout his prophecy, the explanation of some parts of 2:6–10 will need to wait until later. Our present discussion will focus on three particular reversals: the palace, the king, and the treasury.

While Nahum 2:6 continues the account of Nineveh's fall begun in verse 1, the action has turned. While verses 1–5 intermingle accounts of attack and defense, verse 6 marks the demise of the city and verse 7 relates the aftermath. The strongest city of the ancient Near East falls in nine words. We would expect Nahum to provide more detail on this seemingly important subject, but we are also starting to grasp that Nahum did not prophesy according to our expectations. Even the words that he gave do little to explain what happened.

Nahum 2:6 records two events. The river gates are opened and the palace melts. As we have discussed before, Nahum contains water imagery in several places, reinforcing the idea that an abnormal flood has compromised the city walls. Nahum 2:6 suggests that the promise in 1:8 may not be merely figurative: "with an overflowing flood he will make a complete end of the adversaries." An overwhelming flood would also explain the palace melting. The amount of water required to bring down Nineveh's largest structure boggles the mind, however. We have no archaeological evidence of such an inundation.

The flooding mentioned in 1:8 does complement the other storm imagery in the beginning of Nahum. The great palace melting away in the midst of this storm prefigures one of the greatest sermon conclusions ever given. Jesus may have had Nahum 2:6 in mind when he told his parable about two builders.

> Everyone then who hears these words of mine and does them will be like a wise man who built his house on the rock. And the rain fell, and the floods came, and the winds blew and beat on that house, but it did not fall, because it had been founded on the rock. And everyone who hears these words of

mine and does not do them will be like a foolish man who built his house on the sand. And the rain fell, and the floods came, and the winds blew and beat against that house, and it fell, and great was the fall of it. (Matt. 7:24–27)

The Assyrians had used the best possible materials that the world had to offer in order to gird themselves against God's wrath. These proved no stronger than a beach hut in a hurricane.

As a father of seven, I am grateful for all those who use their talents to teach the Bible to children. The popular song about the wise man and the foolish man is not my favorite, however. While useful in helping children to commit these verses to memory, the song does not communicate the gravity of Jesus' words. Many of us have grown up with these lyrics in our mind and have treated a dire warning like a children's story.

As I mentioned before, this parable concludes the Sermon on the Mount. A conclusion seeks to encapsulate the essence of a sermon. It is the "if you remember one thing from this sermon" moment. I do not for a minute want to restrict Jesus to our modern homiletical methods; I merely want you to realize how important this parable is. If, like me, you have to struggle to get children's songs out of your head whenever you read these words, please discipline your mind to see how crucial this is.

In the Sermon on the Mount, Jesus presents two ways of living. A person may live his or her life for the honor of this world or for the honor of Christ. Despite this, much of American evangelicalism seeks to combine the two. Throughout the sermon, however, Jesus destroys that possibility. If you do not know the content of Matthew 5–7 well, I would encourage you to put this book down, find the passage in your Bible, and meditate on it. Pay attention to how Jesus says that you may live before the eyes of man or of God, but not both. Pay attention to how the actions that are commanded in those chapters will lead you to look foolish to almost everyone you know. Pay attention to how seriously Jesus treats the danger of accommodating the world.

A house is built over time. The construction takes place during good weather; it must be built to withstand bad weather. In 2010 and 2011, earthquakes of historic proportions struck two island nations. The 2010 earthquake killed over 160,000 people in Haiti, but the 2011 earthquake and resulting tsunami caused less than one-tenth of this death toll in Japan. Even though the Japanese earthquake hit with much greater force and a tsunami compounded their misery, the Japanese fared better than the Haitians. This may be attributed to better preparation by the Japanese. Their building codes and engineering standards limited the destruction. Probably few nations on earth could have survived such a major disaster so well. In contrast, the lax building standards in Haiti turned many buildings into death traps.

In Matthew 7, Jesus says, "The rain fell, and the floods came" (Matt. 7:27). Vicious storms are coming. I am not foretelling apocalyptic events. They come every day to people all around us, and we just treat them as normal life. Each one of us will face disaster. Only those who spend their lives in preparation will survive with their souls intact. Only if we put Jesus' words into practice will we be able to stand when future events come against us. Teach your children to suffer for Christ at school before you send them to college, or else their faith will not survive college. Discipline yourself to "rejoice and be glad" (Matt. 5:12) when people "revile you and persecute you and utter all kinds of evil against you falsely" (v. 11) for the sake of Christ. If your religious acts and those of your children are not done primarily to earn God's praise—done secretly before his eyes—they will not stand on that day, just as Nineveh did not stand.

A well-built building provides shelter in a storm. A poorly built building will kill its occupants. Assyria placed its hope in worldly power, wealth, and glory. Modern America places its hope in worldly power, wealth, and glory. Jesus calls us away from this life—not because he begrudges us pleasure, but because he knows it will kill us. Come out of the building before it falls. Come into the only "stronghold" that will survive "the day of trouble" (Nah. 1:7).

QUEEN HUZZAB

In 1964, Godfrey Rolles Driver announced the demise of a legendary Assyrian queen in his article "Farewell to Queen Huzzab!"[2] This queen had appeared in the King James Version of the Bible (1611) as the recipient of God's judgment in Nahum 2:7: "And Huzzab shall be led away captive, she shall be brought up, and her maids shall lead her as with the voice of doves, tabering upon their breasts." The men who translated the KJV were brilliant scholars and literary geniuses, but the Hebrew word that begins 2:7 so thoroughly stumped them that they were forced to guess. They transliterated the Hebrew word as a proper name, generating a queen *ex nihilo*. Of all the difficulties in Nahum, this one word has the distinction of being debated the longest. Whereas Nahum's acrostic has dominated Nahum studies for 120 years, the debate about Huzzab extends back more than four hundred. In 1949, one scholar wrote that the issue of Huzzab had consumed "a flood of ink," and "reams of paper have been spent since time immemorial."[3] By 1964, Driver had had enough and declared her demise. His article did not settle the issue, however.[4] It represented a moment of agreement; most scholars now disregard the idea that this is a proper name. There is only negative agreement, though. Without the slightest scrap of evidence that Nahum named a person, few are willing to hold any longer to the King James interpretation. What we still cannot agree upon, however, is what the word does mean. The river of ink continues to flow, and I have the audacity to remove another tree or two in order to present my theory.

118

In verse 7, Nahum turns from structures to people. Once again we are in the situation of trying to deduce identity from ambiguous verbs. In the original Hebrew, the first half of verse 7 contains only three words—all verbs. Once again, the problem arises not because the words are difficult to translate, but because scholars have deemed the resulting translation incomprehensible. Let me illustrate this by showing how a number of popular English translations have dealt with these three words: "Its mistress is stripped; she is carried off" (ESV). "And Huzzab shall be led away captive, she shall be brought up" (KJV). "And it is fixed: She is stripped, she is carried away" (NASB). "It is decreed that the city be exiled and carried away" (NIV). "It is decreed: She shall be led away captive, She shall be brought up" (NKJV). "Nineveh's exile has been decreed" (NLT). "It is decreed that the city be exiled" (NRSV). "Its mistress is stripped, she is carried off" (RSV). This sampling shows that, while there are some similarities among these versions, the translation committees have really struggled to make sense of Nahum's words.

The major difficulty comes because Nahum begins with a third-person masculine verb and then abruptly shifts to two third-person feminine verbs. Again Nahum has failed to tell the reader who "he" and "she" are. Scholars have therefore struggled to know how the first verb relates to the next two. My theory is a simple one. In three words, Nahum has told us the judgment that has befallen both the single male adversary in 1:14 and the single female adversary in 1:11. Furthermore, he leaves their identities ambiguous because he intends the prophecy to describe God's judgment against human rulers, an existing city, and Assyrian deities. In all three chapters of his prophecy, Nahum describes the same judgment. God will incapacitate the male adversary while he pursues and exposes the female one.

Second-semester Hebrew students quickly learn that the New American Standard Version is their friend. While I wouldn't be inclined to read it to my children at bedtime, the translation proves invaluable in working with the original languages. The NASB stays closer to the obvious meaning than the other versions do; it translates the mysterious Huzzab word as "it is fixed." In Hebrew, third-person masculine singular verbs can be translated as "he" or "it," and this translation is perfectly viable. The same verb in a similar form appears in Genesis 28:12 and Judges 9:6. Both passages refer to an inanimate object that has been set up. However, this translation of Nahum 2:7 does not explain what is fixed. I prefer "he is fixed."

Many who know Hebrew much better than I do have rejected this interpretation as nonsensical. In my defense, I offer a different perspective on Nahum's message. We have already seen—and will continue to see—the male enemies of God incapacitated. We have seen Nahum repeatedly refer to them only by general pronouns indicated by the verb form. "He is fixed" fits perfectly within this scheme. The mysterious male figure has lost his motor control—fine and gross—and must be hauled around like furniture. He now faces a punishment that conquered kings have known throughout antiquity: watching helplessly while conquering soldiers punish his family.[5]

The Bible provides an example of this. During Nebuchadnezzar's siege of Jerusalem, King Zedekiah tried to escape from the city. The Babylonians caught him "and brought him up to the king of Babylon at Riblah, and they passed sentence on him" (2 Kings 25:6). The next verse explains the sentence and how it was carried out: "They slaughtered the sons of Zedekiah before his eyes, and put out the eyes of Zedekiah and bound him in chains and took him to Babylon" (2 Kings 25:7). Zedekiah had rebelled against Babylon. How should he be punished? The punishments chosen in this case had several purposes. One was simple vengeance. Such punishments also sent a message to any other king contemplating rebellion. Nebuchadnezzar decided that Zedekiah would stand by helplessly and watch the executions. Then Babylonian soldiers would blind him. This way, the last visual images that entered Zedekiah's brain would be the death of his sons. Zedekiah would always know that his foolish rebellion had brought about this horrific moment, and no images of beauty would later enter his mind to ease the guilt or erase the picture.

After the first verb, the scene shifts to Queen Nineveh. Unfortunately, the rest of this story will need to wait for a later chapter. The punishment of Nineveh's queen in 2:7 finds a fuller expression in 3:4–7. I have devoted two chapters to those four verses, and it would be difficult to explain why she "is stripped" and "carried off" without first working through 3:4–7. Therefore, I ask for your patience until these issues receive a more thorough explanation. Likewise, Nahum develops the themes of 2:7b–8 in the second half of Nahum 3, so an explanation of these verses will also have to wait.

THE BUSINESS OF GATHERING

This brings us to Nahum's command: "Plunder the silver, plunder the gold!" (2:9). Nahum provides many examples of literally fulfilled prophecy. Nineveh had been the treasury for the largest organized crime operation in history. The Assyrians had stolen and extorted the treasures of some of the greatest kingdoms on earth. Immense amounts of wealth had flowed into Nineveh year after year. Despite this, archaeological excavations have uncovered little in the way of precious metals. The soldiers who looted Nineveh obeyed Nahum.

The application of 2:9 extends beyond the idea that the prophets accurately predicted ancient events. Nahum's vision tells a supernatural story as well. This is the battle between the kingdoms of this world and the kingdom of the Lord's Christ. Perhaps no figure in church history fulfilled the command to "plunder the silver, plunder the gold" better than George Müller.

Like many who won great victories for Christ's kingdom, Müller began his life in debauchery; his primary vice was theft. George's father was a tax collector, and George routinely helped himself to portions of these collections. His father's discipline proved useless in curbing this behavior. Müller's autobiography tells many stories about how he stole from anyone and everyone he could, including his closest friends. This compulsion continued as he entered divinity school. He did not fear or love God. He desired the salary and respect that would come from being an influential minister.

Then God converted George Müller. As often happens, God re-formed Müller so that his greatest vice turned into one of his greatest virtues. Soon after Müller's conversion, he decided that he would only ask God for money. As a result, God sent the modern equivalent of $150,000,000 into Müller's coffers over the course of his life—and he handled every penny with impeccable honesty.[6]

Müller understood God's Word regarding money. In our culture of money worship, we desperately need to learn what his life has to teach. Müller's life provides an example of one of God's servants reclaiming silver and gold for the sake of Christ. The following six points highlight a few ways in which Müller demonstrated biblical stewardship to the world.

First, Müller did not love money. "For the love of money is a root of all kinds of evils. It is through this craving that some have wandered away from the faith and pierced themselves with many pangs" (1 Tim. 6:10). This sin had been the taskmaster of his youth, and he would never return to it. He knew what we need to learn. Money has no power to deliver on its false promises. Jesus spoke of "the deceitfulness of riches" (Matt. 13:22). Money promises to solve all problems. It cannot.

Second, Müller knew that he needed money. Money makes a miserable master, but it is a helpful servant. Jesus warned us not to chase money, "for the Gentiles seek after all these things, and your heavenly Father knows that you need them all" (Matt. 6:32). We do need material provision. Müller knew that the ten thousand orphans who came through his doors needed food, clothes, medicine, and heat. God knew it too.

Third, Müller knew the source of money. When God converted him, George Müller ceased using his own striving and manipulation to procure the necessities of life. Instead of stealing from his human father, Müller looked to his heavenly Father for this provision. It is not the pursuit of money that brings destruction. Rather, the method of procuring differentiates the righteous from the unrighteous. "But seek first the kingdom of God and his righteousness, and all these things will be added to you" (Matt. 6:33). God will provide for those who serve him.

Fourth, Müller knew the Bible. "Man shall not live by bread alone, but by every word that comes from the mouth of God" (Matt. 4:4). Müller had a greater need for daily bread than any man of his time. Thousands of hungry mouths depended upon him. Despite this, Müller sought first the food that satisfies for eternity. He is said to have read through the Bible almost two hundred times.

Fifth, Müller knew how to pray. The life of George Whitefield had an early impact on him. Particularly "that Whitefield's unparalleled success in evangelistic labours was plainly traceable to two causes and could not be separated from them as direct effects; namely, his *unusual prayerfulness, and his habit of reading the Bible on his knees.*"[7] All of the money that Müller received came in answer to prayer. Müller knew how to wrestle in prayer, and his writings become repetitive because they chronicled hundreds upon hundreds of stories of him praying and receiving just what he asked for.

Sixth—and most importantly—Müller's purpose for asking was God's glory. He did not primarily set out to feed orphans. As a pastor, he observed how the people in his congregation lived lives "choked by the cares and riches and pleasures of life" (Luke 8:14). The care of orphans was a mere by-product of Müller's greatest desire: "That God may be glorified, should He be pleased to furnish me with the means, in its being seen that it is not a vain thing to trust in Him; and that thus the faith of His children may be strengthened."[8] The orphanages were meant to be a visible testimony that God would provide for his people.

Nineveh had stockpiled the wealth of the ancient Near East. They had stolen it from Israel, Judah, and the other surrounding nations. The vast treasures of Elam, Babylon, and Egypt had poured in. Nahum 2:9 shows that God does not desire his people to go without their daily necessities. He also does not want his people to lack the resources needed to carry on his work. When Israel and Judah became obsessed with their own luxury, God removed their wealth. The book of Amos, for instance, recounts the story of Israel's economic injustice. A humble people, however, will receive all that they need for their own provision and to care for others.

Ecclesiastes 2:26 says, "For to the one who pleases him God has given wisdom and knowledge and joy, but to the sinner he has given the business of gathering and collecting, only to give to one who pleases God." Nineveh had performed God's financial plan in two ways. It removed the wealth from God's people when they sought to find their lives through it. Nineveh also did the work of gathering, so that God could give it back.

The treasure that Assyria gathered went to Media and Babylon when Nineveh fell. The treasure of Media and Babylon became the wealth of Persia. The wealth of Persia rebuilt Jerusalem. God waited, though, until two men humbled themselves, fasted, and reminded God of his written promises. Like Müller, Ezra and Nehemiah knew that "there is no end of the treasure or of the wealth of all precious things" (Nah. 2:9) for the one who desires it for God's glory and will use God's means to get his provision.

Müller's life demonstrated God's faithfulness, not his own righteousness. The lessons of church history show that

God will fulfill his Word. He has promised to provide what we need as we seek to do his will. God had told Müller that "all that is mine is yours" (Luke 15:31). He had also given Müller the ability to believe this. God asks us to walk in faith, trusting him to supply our material needs as we seek to obey his calling in our lives. Christ exchanged the wealth of heaven for rags on earth: "For you know the grace of our Lord Jesus Christ, that though he was rich, yet for your sake he became poor, so that you by his poverty might become rich" (2 Cor. 8:9). The life of Christ serves as the greatest example that we may trust God with our finances. "He who did not spare his own Son but gave him up for us all, how will he not also with him graciously give us all things?" (Rom. 8:32).

FOR FURTHER REFLECTION

1. Read 1 Samuel 2:1–10 and Luke 1:46–55. What similarities do you see between these two prayers? How do these prayers relate to the theme of reversal? To what extent do you behave as if God will actually intervene to bring the proud low and exalt the humble?

2. Jesus started the parable of the wise and the foolish builders with the words, "Everyone then who hears these words of mine and does them . . ." (Matt. 7:24). What actions does Jesus refer to?

3. James commands us,

> Be doers of the word, and not hearers only, deceiving yourselves. For if anyone is a hearer of the word and not a doer, he is like a man who looks intently at his natural face in a mirror. For he looks at himself and goes away and at once forgets what he was like. (James 1:22–24)

Read through Matthew 5–7. Have you been primarily a "doer" or just a "hearer" of these words?

4. Reread the six principles that guided George Müller with respect to money. Which one(s) do you find most difficult? Spend some time in prayer, asking God to give you a biblical view of money.

5. How did Jesus relate to money? Why is his righteousness good news for you with respect to money, as it is in every other matter?

CHAPTER NINE

THE GOOD SHEPHERD (2:11–13)

I am the good shepherd. The good shepherd lays down his life for the sheep. (John 10:11)

In the midst of his sermon—moments before his death—the martyr Stephen gave us a remarkable insight into the Minor Prophets. He introduced a quote from Amos 5:25 with the words "as it is written in the book of the prophets" (Acts 7:42). Here, Stephen speaks by inspiration of God and labels the Minor Prophets as one book, not twelve. Therefore, the Minor Prophets become another piece in the Christian puzzle. How can distinct units function as a unity? In Scripture, the book of Psalms serves as the easiest example of this. We talk of individual psalms and a book of Psalms. Each psalm functions as a distinct unit. Each one contributes to the book as a whole. Even within the book of Psalms we find five divisions (Pss. 1–41; 42–72; 73–89; 90–106; 107–150). The book of Psalms has been divided into five different books since before the birth of Christ. We have only the faintest understanding of the meaning of these divisions. Many other examples exist. Both the Old and New Testaments form distinct units, yet they also come together as a whole, dependent upon each other. Consider how we would read Job or Song of Solomon differently if these books were not part of Scripture. How does putting Esther in the context of the New Testament affect its meaning? Of course, these difficulties extend into theological realities that defy comprehension. We hold that Jesus is fully God and fully man, yet we must admit that this is beyond understanding. How can Jesus be the Word? How can the Word become flesh? Finally, perhaps the most profound theological mystery is that "in the unity of the Godhead there be three persons, of one substance, power, and eternity" (WCF 2.3). Our minds struggle to understand how so many aspects of Christianity involve distinct entities that form one unity.

Besides Stephen, many other ancient witnesses state—implicitly or explicitly—that the Minor Prophets form one book. These include anonymous scribes, intertestamental literature, the Talmud, Josephus, and early church fathers. Unfortunately, while all these witnesses treat the Minor Prophets as a unity, not one of them explains the nature of this unity. Numerous theories try to explain how the books relate to each other, but these remain speculative. Hopefully, future insight will come.

Since the Minor Prophets form one book, their order matters. One book leads into the next. Each book affects the context of the next one. This has particular relevance for the text before us. In the book of the Twelve Prophets, the promise that God will destroy the Assyrian "lions" (Nah. 2:11–13) comes just a few chapters after Micah prophesies that a shepherd will "shepherd the land of Assyria with the sword" (Mic. 5:6).

MICAH 5

While most portions of the Minor Prophets remain obscure in modern churches, Micah 5 does receive attention—at least around Christmastime. It contains the prophecy that the Christ would be born in Bethlehem. Because of this passage, Herod knew where to look for the child "who

has been born king of the Jews" (Matt. 2:2). It pronounces
a profound reversal.

> Now muster your troops, O daughter of troops;
>   siege is laid against us;
> with a rod they strike the judge of Israel
>   on the cheek.
> But you, O Bethlehem Ephrathah,
>   who are too little to be among the clans of Judah,
> from you shall come forth for me
>   one who is to be ruler in Israel,
> whose coming forth is from of old,
>   from ancient days.
> Therefore he shall give them up until the time
>   when she who is in labor has given birth;
> then the rest of his brothers shall return
>   to the people of Israel.
> And he shall stand and shepherd his flock in the
>   strength of the Lord,
>   in the majesty of the name of the Lord his God.
> And they shall dwell secure, for now he shall be great
>   to the ends of the earth.
> And he shall be their peace.
>
> When the Assyrian comes into our land
>   and treads in our palaces,
> then we will raise against him seven shepherds
>   and eight princes of men;
> they shall shepherd the land of Assyria with the sword,
>   and the land of Nimrod at its entrances;
> and he shall deliver us from the Assyrian
>   when he comes into our land
>   and treads within our border. (Mic. 5:1–6)

First, Micah 5 reverses geography. Bethlehem becomes
great as Assyria falls. This town, so obscure that Micah must
clarify which Bethlehem he means, gives rise to Israel's

empire. Even though Bethlehem did not merit acclaim in Judah, it would bring forth the king of the earth. Second, Micah 5 reverses empires. The shepherds of Israel will rule Assyria. God led his people into "a good and broad land, a land flowing with milk and honey" (Ex. 3:8), but he also placed his people in a precarious position. Israel occupied a piece of land desired for its strategic position and trade routes. The powerful peoples that surrounded Israel—Egyptians, Babylonians, and Assyrians—would always contend for this land. Besides the major powers, lesser nations such as Philistia, Edom, and Aram would also vie with Israel for local supremacy. Micah 5 says that not only would Israel be free from Assyrian rule, it would rule Assyria. Third, Micah 5 reverses heroes. The one born in Bethlehem would conquer the Assyrian.

NIMROD

Micah 5 prophesies that our savior from Bethlehem would contend with "the Assyrian" (5:5). This Hebrew word matches the name of Assyria's patriarch Asshur, whom we find in Genesis 10:22. Asshur will receive more attention in the final chapter of this book. Micah 5:6 also calls Assyria "the land of Nimrod." This Nimrod "was the first on earth to be a mighty man. He was a mighty hunter before the LORD" (Gen. 10:8–9). According to Micah 5, Assyria's rebellion against God goes back to the times of these two mighty men. They founded cities and civilizations. They used their great intellects and prowess to build the first empires.

Genesis 10 calls Nimrod a mighty hunter before the Lord because God gave him skill with weapons. God's people needed those who could defend them against the wild beasts and could provide food. Instead, Nimrod used his gifts for military conquest. He subjugated peoples to his will. Micah 5 prophesied that the Christ would undo this legacy. Nahum 2:11–13 did also.

LIONS

In 2:11, Nahum uses one of his favorite poetic devices. The repetition in this verse emphasizes the lionlike nature of Assyria. In one sentence, we find "lions' den," "young lions," "lion and lioness," and "cubs." The metaphor fits Assyria well for several reasons. First, Assyria lived as the top predator of its day. Second, lions lived in Assyria at that time. Third, and most importantly, Assyrian ideology used the metaphor as well. Assyrian kings boasted of their physical prowess by describing their lion-hunting exploits.[1] The parking lot of my local Walmart provides me with weekly reminders that many people correlate hunting with manhood. If some find their masculine identity by using rifles to hunt deer, how much more those who chased lions with spears? They did this not only for the prestige of strapping the huge cats to their chariots, but also to mark themselves as protectors of the people. Ashurbanipal—the Assyrian king of Nahum's day—made more use of this image than any of his predecessors had. Assyrian artists carved stone reliefs celebrating these lion hunts for his palace.

Nahum 2:11–13 takes these boasts and turns them on their head. Instead of Ashurbanipal being the great king who hunts lions to protect his people, Nahum switches these roles. First, Ashurbanipal may not boast in being the greatest of men, for he is but a beast, living by his passions. Second, he does not protect his people but devours them. They exist for his pleasure, glory, and consumption.

By contrast, the Christ from Micah 5 will "stand and shepherd his flock in the strength of the LORD, in the majesty of the name of the LORD his God. And they shall dwell secure, for now he shall be great to the ends of the earth. And he shall be their peace" (Mic. 5:4–5). This Christ would teach his followers,

> You know that those who are considered rulers of
> the Gentiles lord it over them, and their great ones

exercise authority over them. But it shall not be so among you. But whoever would be great among you must be your servant, and whoever would be first among you must be slave of all. For even the Son of Man came not to be served but to serve, and to give his life as a ransom for many. (Mark 10:42–45)

Some use their authority for the benefit of others. Many more use their authority primarily for their own pleasure and glory. Ashurbanipal fell firmly in the latter group. Unfortunately, he also ruled the largest empire the world had ever seen, and he delighted in cruelty. Micah prophesied the end of such Assyrian kings. Nahum declared the prophecy fulfilled.

THE SHEPHERD-KING

Perhaps you are a pastor. If not, you likely have a pastor. The title *pastor* comes from the Latin word (curiously enough) *pastor*, which means "shepherd." The correlation between ministry and shepherding runs throughout Scripture. The first man who was murdered for his faith shepherded sheep (Gen. 4:2). Abraham, Moses, and David all roamed the wilderness with their livestock at one time. Jesus reinstated Peter by commanding him, "Feed my sheep" (John 21:17). The modern conception of shepherds does not do justice to Micah 5, however. "When the Assyrian comes into our land and treads in our palaces, then we will raise against him seven shepherds and eight princes of men; they shall shepherd the land of Assyria with the sword, and the land of Nimrod at its entrances; and he shall deliver us from the Assyrian when he comes into our land and treads within our border" (Mic. 5:5–6). The shepherds in Micah's day stood between their sheep and ferocious beasts. The job was not for the timid. It involved life-threatening experiences with the dangers of nature. For this reason, the boy David was not afraid of Goliath:

> Your servant used to keep sheep for his father. And when there came a lion, or a bear, and took a lamb from the flock, I went after him and struck him and delivered it out of his mouth. And if he arose against me, I caught him by his beard and struck him and killed him. Your servant has struck down both lions and bears, and this uncircumcised Philistine shall be like one of them. (1 Sam. 17:34–36)

Micah's Bethlehemite would raise up such shepherds from the birthplace of David. They would face these lions of Assyria armed with swords, not staffs.

When Nahum prophesied the demise of these lions, he mixed his metaphor, intertwining lion imagery with chariots and messengers. In 2:13, God promised the ambiguous female figure that he would "burn your chariots in smoke, and the sword shall devour your young lions. I will cut off your prey from the earth, and the voice of your messengers shall no longer be heard." This verse reinforces the incapacitation prophesied in 1:9–12. First, God destroys Nineveh's chariot. The chariot served as Assyria's primary weapon. The burning of the chariot indicates the loss of military prowess and mobility. Second, there will be no offspring. The line will die out. Indeed, Assyria would have no competent kings once Ashurbanipal died. Third, God will remove Assyria's sustenance. As top predators, lions face a daunting challenge. They must continually hunt, lest they starve. Since God has cut off the Assyrian game, the predatory military will languish and die. Fourth, the messengers will no longer go forth to taunt and demand. No more will ancient peoples suffer through the terror induced by insolent emissaries.

This shepherding by the sword contradicts the typical interpretation of Nahum. Shepherds do not primarily hunt.

They feed, care for, and protect sheep. Killing becomes necessary only when a predator intends to harm the sheep. The words of Micah 5 and Nahum 2 pronounce God's desire to rid Assyria of these predators. The Old Testament speaks of Assyria's redemption, not Assyria's destruction. If we read Nahum carefully and put aside our preconceptions about the book, we see how this redemption took place. God destroyed Assyria's rulers—both supernatural and human—who consumed its people. God replaced these evil beings with humble yet powerful shepherds who would care for the flock. God desired that the Assyrians would find refuge in him, free from their carnivorous kings.

The shepherd imagery that runs throughout the Old Testament finds its culmination in Jesus. He declared himself the fulfillment of each of these texts when he said, "I am the good shepherd" (John 10:11). Hopefully, the above treatment of Micah and Nahum will allow you to read these words in a new light. I encourage you at this point to put down this book and meditate on the entire chapter of John 10. See how Jesus describes himself as the one who "lays down his life for the sheep" (10:11), as opposed to the hired man who runs away (10:12-13) or the thief who "comes only to steal and kill and destroy" (10:10). We have few authority figures in our lives who will protect us when facing danger to themselves. If they do not seek to devour us, they will often run rather than risk harm to themselves.

Any who would come in Jesus' name must likewise give themselves for the sheep. We are not here to receive the glory due to Jesus. Rather, we are here so that others may see Jesus' beauty and glory for themselves and may worship him. We may do this fearlessly because we know that Jesus is our Good Shepherd. He protects and feeds us so that his love may flow through us to others. We dare not use God's people to establish our own reputation. Instead, we must take up our sword to do battle with any who would desecrate Christ's bride.

We need to rediscover Micah's model of ministry. The job of pastor involves strength and danger. While one may apply this teaching to many aspects of ministry, I will limit myself to addressing two specific ways in which a pastor must imperil himself for his congregation. I believe that each of these has fallen into disuse and that Christ's people suffer for it. First, a pastor must learn to rebuke those within the church who threaten its people. This theme occurs repeatedly in the Pastoral Epistles (the letters that Paul wrote to pastors). For instance, Titus 1:9 says that a pastor "must hold firm to the trustworthy word as taught, so that he may be able to give instruction in sound doctrine and also to rebuke those who contradict it." Titus 1:13 says, "Therefore rebuke them sharply, that they may be sound in the faith." Titus 2:15 says, "Exhort and rebuke with all authority." I remember reading that last passage one day and realizing that my seminary professors had taught me how to "exhort" but not how to "rebuke."

I did find excellent instruction on this topic from John Bunyan. In *Pilgrim's Progress*, Christian and Faithful join company to walk along the narrow path to the Celestial City. They soon meet Talkative. Bunyan describes Talkative as a man who "talketh of prayer, of repentance, of faith, and of the new birth; but he knows but only to talk of them."[2] Faithful and Talkative enter into an extended conversation that ends with Faithful confronting Talkative with his hypocrisy, causing Talkative to leave their company. Bunyan closes this encounter with the following interchange:

Faithful: But I am glad we had this little discourse with him, it may happen that he will think of it again; however, I have dealt plainly with him, and so am clear of his blood if he perisheth.

Christian: You did well to talk so plainly to him as you did. There is but little of this faithful dealing with men now-a-days, and that makes religion to stink so in the nostrils of many as it doth; for they are these talkative fools, whose religion is only in word, and who are debauched and vain in their conversation, that (being so much admitted into the fellowship of the godly) do puzzle the world, blemish Christianity, and grieve the sincere. I wish that all men would deal with such as you have done; then should they either be made more conformable to religion, or the company of saints would be too hot for them.[3]

If there was "little of this faithful dealing with men" in Bunyan's day, I suspect that the lack has only increased in our own day. This passage struck me deeply, as I have routinely shied away from confronting people for fear that they would respond as Talkative did. We may justify this cowardice in a way that still preserves our appearance of godliness. We may say that we desire to keep peace and unity in the church, but an honest reading of the New Testament will not let this stand. A pastor who will not confront sin and heresy abandons Christ's people to the wolves in their midst. Since those "who teach will be judged with greater strictness" (James 3:1), such ministers will have much to answer for on the day of judgment.

Second, the First Epistle of Peter makes a direct reference to Micah and Nahum when it says,

Be sober-minded; be watchful. Your adversary the devil prowls around like a roaring lion, seeking someone to devour. Resist him, firm in your faith, knowing that the same kinds of suffering are being experienced by your brotherhood throughout the world. (1 Peter 5:8–9)

Peter confirmed what Jesus had already indicated. The greatest adversary that the sheep face is Satan. Since Satan hunts us, we must be "sober-minded" and "watchful." It stands to reason that if we ignore this command, Satan will succeed in his mission. The Bible has given us a dire warning and coupled it with firm instruction. We dare not ignore this. Unfortunately, few pastors know how to "wrestle . . . against the rulers, against the authorities, against the cosmic powers over this present darkness, against the spiritual forces of evil in the heavenly places" (Eph. 6:12). Most pastors are overworked. Many are burned out. They work long hours, doing everything but wrestling in prayer for the souls of their people. We have reaped what we have sown. If a congregation wants a man who will fight for their souls and the souls of their children, they must look for a man who knows how to fight with the Devil, who knows how to pray. If you are such an overworked pastor who does not know how to stand between Satan and Jesus' sheep, I encourage you to humble yourself before God and confess that you have spent your time doing things expected of you by people and have ignored the things expected of you by God. I call upon you to have the courage to disappoint the expectations of the congregation, so that you may do the things that they most need. The Bible gives the pastor his job description: to "devote" himself "to prayer and to the ministry of the word" (Acts 6:4). You must choose between fulfilling the expectations of man and fulfilling those of God. If you would truly battle for the souls in your midst, you must learn how to shepherd with a sword.

FOR FURTHER REFLECTION

1. Read Psalm 23. In what ways has Jesus been your shepherd? How has he restored your soul (v. 3)? How has your life been different, knowing his shepherding care? If you have not known Jesus as a shepherd, will you submit to him now and ask him to shepherd you?

2. Read Ezekiel 34. What does Ezekiel teach about biblical shepherds? How does Ezekiel 34 relate to Micah 5 and Nahum 2?

3. Do you know how to "wrestle . . . against the rulers, against the authorities, against the cosmic powers over this present darkness, against the spiritual forces of evil in the heavenly places" (Eph. 6:12) for the souls of those around you? If not, pray to God that he would train and equip you for this battle.

CHAPTER TEN

THE SHADOW OF DEATH (3:1–3)

Even though I walk through the valley
of the shadow of death,
I will fear no evil,
for you are with me. (Ps. 23:4)

Even though Assyrian tyranny and brutality troubled the ancient Near East off and on for over a thousand years, Nahum lived under the most violent king that Assyria ever produced. One renowned Assyriologist put it this way:

> Earlier Assyrian kings had been harsh, yes, ruthless. Where there was rebellion, they crushed it; where opposition, they destroyed it. But only Ashurbanipal put vindictiveness on display; only he slashed the face of a dead enemy, desecrated tombs of the dead he had not been able to punish when living, spared the lives of captive kings that he might humiliate them better living than dead. It is not the historian's part to lay blame, but the historian must record; and malice as a driving force behind the later Ashurbanipal is a fact of history.[1]

Reading Assyrian annals is not for the queasy. Assyrian kings boasted and reveled in their victories. Again, though,

Ashurbanipal stands out. One of his inscriptions reads, "I pierced his cheeks with the sharp-edged spear, my personal weapon, by laying the very hands on him which I had received to conquer opposition against me; I put the ring to his jaw, placed a dog collar around his neck and made him guard the bar of the east gate of Nineveh."[2] Another says, "The wheels of my war chariot, which brings low the wicked and evil, were bespattered with blood and filth. With the bodies of their warriors I filled the plain, like grass. (Their) testicles I cut off, and tore out their privates."[3] Ashurbanipal's Assyria systematized brutal warfare beyond what the world had previously witnessed. Unfortunately, many nations would later eclipse Assyria in this regard.

If the accounts above were difficult to read, I apologize for putting them in. At the same time, we must grasp the scale and degree of Assyrian barbarity that Nahum addressed. Many have dismissed or disdained Nahum because of the violence mentioned in the book. Unfortunately, these readers often fail to distinguish between Nahum's descriptions of Assyria and his judgments against Assyria.

Nahum prophesied the fall of Nineveh. The city endured a four-month siege before invaders breached its walls and razed it in 612 B.C. Undoubtedly the Ninevites suffered unimaginable horrors as the soldiers from Babylon and Media vented their fury. According to Nahum, though, the "hosts of slain, heaps of corpses, dead bodies without end" in 3:3 were not the people whom the Babylonians killed. Nahum says they were "all for the countless whorings of the prostitute" (Nah. 3:4). The piles of bodies in verse 3 were the victims of Assyria, rather than Assyrians themselves.[4]

WOE

The Hebrew prophets spoke God's word mainly to Israel and Judah. The author of Hebrews began the epistle by explaining, "Long ago, at many times and in many ways, God spoke to our fathers by the prophets, but in these last days he has spoken to us by his Son" (Heb. 1:1–2). The prophets served as intermediaries. They received God's word and communicated it to his people.

Many of the prophetic books, however, contain sections of judgment against other nations. Each of the major prophets—Isaiah, Jeremiah, and Ezekiel—contains long sections in which the prophet pronounces oracles of woe on foreign peoples. Some of the Minor Prophets do as well. The exact boundaries of these oracles against the nations are disputed, but no one disputes that Nahum belongs in the category.

When Nahum 3:1 begins with the word "woe," it places what comes next within a specific genre. The Hebrew word occurs fifty times in the Old Testament prophets. Often it places a curse on the recipient, as it does in Nahum.

Nahum's curse came because of three crimes. The prophet charged Nineveh with breaking the sixth, eighth, and ninth commandments. The men of Nineveh had murdered, stolen, and lied—on a multinational scale.

The enormity of these crimes makes the following statement by Jesus astonishing: "The men of Nineveh will rise up at the judgment with this generation and condemn it, for they repented at the preaching of Jonah, and behold, something greater than Jonah is here" (Matt. 12:41). A chapter earlier, Matthew's gospel records another statement at least as shocking.

> Then [Jesus] began to denounce the cities where most of his mighty works had been done, because they did not repent. "Woe to you, Chorazin! Woe to you, Bethsaida! For if the mighty works done in you had been done in Tyre and Sidon, they would have repented long ago in sackcloth and ashes. But I tell you, it will be more bearable on the day of judgment for Tyre and Sidon than for you. And you,

Capernaum, will you be exalted to heaven? You will be brought down to Hades. For if the mighty works done in you had been done in Sodom, it would have remained until this day. But I tell you that it will be more tolerable on the day of judgment for the land of Sodom than for you." (Matt. 11:20–24)

As recorded in these two chapters, Jesus compared his hearers to four of the most infamous cities of ancient times. To the dismay of his listeners, he condemned them as the greater sinners.

When we add the crimes of Sodom to those listed in Nahum 3:1, we have two societies responsible for some of the most egregious breaches of the sixth, seventh, eighth, and ninth commandments that are recorded in the Bible. We cannot imagine the horror or anger that Jesus' audience must have felt in hearing these words. On what basis could Jesus have made this claim? What standard did Jesus use to rate one sin higher than another? In all four cases—Nineveh, Tyre, Sidon, and Sodom—Jesus stated that the advantage lay in their willingness to repent, should Jesus have preached there. Of the four, only one of the cities had repented. The Bible records the reason that Nineveh repented: "And the people of Nineveh believed God" (Jonah 3:5).

In contrast, Israel refused to believe Jesus. This hardness only increased throughout his ministry. Because of this, Jesus too took on the prophetic role of preaching a sermon of woe. Matthew 23 records this series of seven woes against the scribes and Pharisees. This chapter repeatedly reinforces what Jesus' earlier statements of woe had already declared—that offenses against Christ and the gospel come under greater judgment than offenses committed against humanity.

The sin of hypocrisy comes under particularly severe censure. We are used to reading these words in the Bible and shaking our heads at the Pharisees. In recent decades, the church has received criticism for this from those who argue that the Pharisees were not really that bad. We have given little answer—not because the Pharisees were not so bad, but because we are no better. We have to redefine hypocrisy because Jesus' definition fits the spiritual state of our nation so well. We start with the assumption that Jesus' words in Matthew 23 could not refer to us, and so we escape the obvious conclusion. Matthew 11, 12, and 23 do speak directly to us, though. Jesus' statements of woe speak to our condition. Every day we do the same things that they did. Like the Pharisees of Jesus' day, we would rather pick different commandments and consider those who break them as greater sinners than those who pretend to be righteous in order to impress men.

We must stop doing that. We must let the law do its job. "Now we know that whatever the law says it speaks to those who are under the law, so that every mouth may be stopped, and the whole world may be held accountable to God" (Rom. 3:19). Jesus spoke these woes to silence us. Instead of explaining away our sin or justifying ourselves "before men" (Luke 16:15), we must come to God humbly, admit our guilt, and call out for Christ's forgiveness and cleansing of such evil.

The Assyrians committed wholesale slaughter. They found pleasure and identity in their breaking of God's commandment, "You shall not murder" (Ex. 20:13). Yet the Jerusalemites of Jesus' day committed a much greater offense against the sixth commandment. Religious hypocrisy will feed all other sins: "sexual immorality, impurity, sensuality, idolatry, sorcery, enmity, strife, jealousy, fits of anger, rivalries, dissensions, divisions, envy, drunkenness, orgies, and things like these" (Gal. 5:19–21). In the case of Jesus' countrymen, it led to them murdering the Son of God. If we rely on observing the law, we come under a curse (Gal. 3:10). If we strive for our own righteousness, we will have to lie to ourselves and lie to others. If we allow this hypocrisy to persist, it will drive us into deeper and deeper depravity.

Would you be free from the burden of sin?
There's pow'r in the blood, pow'r in the blood;
Would you o'er evil a victory win?
There's wonderful pow'r in the blood.[5]

The only means of deliverance from Jesus' woes is confession and repentance. As the next stanza of the hymn says,

Would you be free from your passion and pride?
There's pow'r in the blood, pow'r in the blood;
Come for a cleansing to Calvary's tide;
There's wonderful pow'r in the blood.[6]

Please, have the courage to admit your hypocrisy. Have the wisdom to see how grievously evil it is. Have the sense to go to the cross for cleansing. Nothing else can help. Your every striving in the flesh to fix yourself has made it worse.

Cast your deadly "doing" down—
Down at Jesus' feet;
Stand in Him, in Him alone,
Gloriously complete.[7]

NINEVEH AS HELL

After spending almost half of this chapter on one word, I will now speed up by looking at Nahum 3:1–3 as a whole. I believe that Nahum used these verses to portray Nineveh as a city of the dead. He alluded to both biblical and Assyrian concepts of the underworld.

Assyria shared a common culture with Babylon. Many of the mythic stories of Mesopotamia pertained to gods and goddesses common to both nations. One uniquely Assyrian myth may perhaps help to explain why Nahum 3:3 tells us about so many dead bodies.

"The Netherworld Vision of an Assyrian Crown Prince" tells the "oldest known visionary journey to hell" by a human being.[8] It recounts the story of an Assyrian crown prince who voluntarily visits the underworld after a period of personal crisis. The myth does not name this crown prince, but Ashurbanipal is the best candidate.[9] Nergal, the chief god of the Mesopotamian underworld, does not appreciate the intrusion and is about to smash Ashurbanipal's skull with a scepter. The prince is understandably terrified. Then Nergal's wise advisor counsels him to let the prince go, in order to help Nergal's public relations on earth. The god concurs and lets the prince go after the prince vows to do so. If this myth stemmed from Ashurbanipal, Nahum's emperor had a special association with the god of the dead.

I find this possibility interesting, but it remains speculative. I mention it here because Nahum contains quite a bit of underworld imagery. Whether or not it alludes to "The Netherworld Vision," Nahum's own vision certainly uses imagery of hell.

The doctrine of hell finds much clearer expression in the New Testament than in the Old. Much of what we do know about hell came directly from the lips of Jesus. The Old Testament does speak about "the grave" and "Sheol." One such passage from Isaiah helps us to understand Nahum's multiple references to Nineveh's voracious appetite for plunder (2:9), "torn flesh" (2:12), and dead bodies (3:3). According to Isaiah, "Sheol has enlarged its appetite and opened its mouth beyond measure" (Isa. 5:14). Nineveh consumes and keeps. It lets nothing leave.

The reference to God's pursuing "his enemies into darkness" (Nah. 1:8) also uses the imagery of Sheol. Several biblical passages use darkness as a description of Sheol. For example:

> Are not my days few?
>   Then cease, and leave me alone, that I may find
>   a little cheer

before I go—and I shall not return—
   to the land of darkness and deep shadow,
the land of gloom like thick darkness,
   like deep shadow without any order,
   where light is as thick darkness. (Job 10:20–22)

Psalm 88 speaks many times of the land of the dead. The psalmist seems to despair from beginning to end. In verse 6, he says, "You have put me in the depths of the pit, in the regions dark and deep."

Nineveh's "gates" (2:6; 3:13) and "bars" (3:13) also suggest Sheol, as Hezekiah's lament demonstrates.

I said, In the middle of my days
   I must depart;
I am consigned to the gates of Sheol
   for the rest of my years.
I said, I shall not see the LORD,
   the LORD in the land of the living;
I shall look on man no more
   among the inhabitants of the world. (Isa. 38:10–11)

Jonah also describes his impending death in such a way.

The waters closed in over me to take my life;
   the deep surrounded me;
weeds were wrapped about my head
   at the roots of the mountains.
I went down to the land
   whose bars closed upon me forever;
yet you brought up my life from the pit,
   O LORD my God. (Jonah 2:5–6)

Once a human descends to the land of the dead, gates and bars lock behind him.

NAHUM 3:14-15

Two more verses of Nahum deserve consideration in this discussion. In a taunt against the female enemy, the prophet commands, "Draw water for the siege; strengthen your forts; go into the clay; tread the mortar; take hold of the brick mold! There will the fire devour you; the sword will cut you off. It will devour you like the locust" (Nah. 3:14-15). These verses contain historical and supernatural imagery. The activities of 3:14 fit the actions of a Mesopotamian city preparing for a siege. The city would store as much water as possible. Its inhabitants would inspect the defenses and reinforce any weaknesses. Since Assyria lacked large trees and quarries, they tended to build with mud brick. Therefore, the citizens would gather clay, mold it into bricks, and fire it in the kiln.

These verses also use strong underworld imagery. In Mesopotamian myth, the inhabitants of the land of the dead eat dust and clay. In fact, the myths *The Epic of Gilgamesh*, "Nergal and Ersihkal," and "The Descent of Ishtar into the Underworld" all contain a nearly identical description of the underworld that includes all of the above-mentioned traits. "The Descent of Ishtar into the Underworld" says,

> To the house which those who enter cannot leave,
> On the road where travelling is one-way only,
> To the house where those who enter are deprived
> of light,
> Where dust is their food, clay their bread.
> They see no light, they dwell in darkness,
> They are clothed like birds, with feathers.
> Over the door and the bolt, dust has settled.[10]

The underworld consumes, does not allow its inhabitants out, feeds souls with clay, keeps them in darkness, and bars them in.

The words of Nahum 3:15 fit even better with Jesus' description of hell in Mark 9:48. In this verse, Jesus quotes

Isaiah 66:24 and teaches that "where their worm does not die and the fire is not quenched" refers to hell. Nineveh experienced literal "fire" and "sword" (Nah. 3:15) when the Babylonians took the city. It experienced the onslaught of figurative locusts as the Medes removed everything of value. Jesus applies these words to a more horrific end. He warns us to take any step necessary to avoid this eternity.

THE DOCTRINE OF HELL TODAY

The doctrine of hell has fallen into disfavor. Many preachers, churches, and denominations have chosen either to openly deny God's eternal judgment or just to ignore it. We do not have the option to change God's message to suit our culture, however. He has charged us to speak plainly. We may make people angry. We may lose friends. We may lose church members. Yet we do not have the option of dancing around or ignoring the issue of hell. We have been charged with a message to deliver. We must deliver it. That message includes eternal punishment for all who will not submit to Christ as Lord. We do the world no favors by shirking this duty. They may hate us, but they desperately need to know the truth.

God has ordained fear of judgment as one means by which people will respond to the gospel. Perhaps the most famous sermon ever delivered in English proves this point. Until recently, high school literature classes included a study of "Sinners in the Hands of an Angry God," a sermon by Jonathan Edwards. I read it in my public high school. My teacher had little use for its doctrine, but she acknowledged it as a fine work of literature and a turning point in American history. Edwards said,

> The use of this awful subject may be for awakening unconverted persons in this congregation. This that you have heard is the case of every one of you that

148

are out of Christ.—That world of misery, that lake of burning brimstone, is extended abroad under you. There is the dreadful pit of the glowing flames of the wrath of God; there is hell's wide gaping mouth open; and you have nothing to stand upon, nor any thing to take hold of; there is nothing between you and hell but the air; it is only the power and mere pleasure of God that holds you up.[11]

Our modern preaching lacks words like these, not because we love men more, but because we love them less. Edwards had the privilege of witnessing powerful revivals. He also had the experience of constant slander, eventually losing his pulpit. Only a man who loved God and agonized over souls could preach like this. Too often, the fear of man constrains our preaching more than the fear of God does.

The necessity of preaching God's wrath may also be seen in the greatest systematic expression of the gospel. You may be familiar with "the Romans Road." Some of the first Bible verses that I memorized, and perhaps that you memorized, were Romans 3:23; 6:23; 10:9. Paul's logical development of the doctrine of salvation makes it an excellent place to teach evangelism and understand the doctrines of grace. Well, how did the greatest missionary, evangelist, and theologian (besides Jesus) begin his gospel presentation? If you read Romans, you will find introductory remarks, a statement about the gospel's power, and then sixty-three verses about God's wrath against wickedness. This section begins by saying, "For the wrath of God is revealed from heaven against all ungodliness and unrighteousness of men, who by their unrighteousness suppress the truth" (Rom. 1:18). It ends by stating, "Now we know that whatever the law says it speaks to those who are under the law, so that every mouth may be stopped, and the whole world may be held accountable to God" (Rom 3:19). The purpose of every verse in between is to convince the reader that all stand condemned under God's righteous judgment.

If we ignore the teaching of Scripture, the example of Scripture, and the evidence of church history, what hope do we have of convincing sinners to repent, if we do not first show them the wickedness of their sins, the holiness of God, and the wrath that is coming? I will answer: none. Our words will have no power, no blessing of God, and no authority from the Holy Spirit.

If the above argument has not convinced you of the importance of teaching on hell, let me add one more Bible passage. "If I say to the wicked, 'You shall surely die,' and you give him no warning, nor speak to warn the wicked from his wicked way, in order to save his life, that wicked person shall die for his iniquity, but his blood I will require at your hand" (Ezek. 3:18). If we will not warn people of their impending doom out of a desire for God's glory or for their salvation, perhaps we will do so merely from the fear of God. I do not know what would be involved in God's requiring the blood of a sinner at my hand, but it sounds terrible. If we do not discount these words as hyperbole, they must call us to repentance. In Paul's farewell sermon to the Ephesians, he claimed, "I am innocent of the blood of all" (Acts 20:26). I can make no such boast. I have not been nearly so faithful. Perhaps this is true of you as well. I have asked many times for forgiveness. I ask you to examine this issue in your own life.

I do not want to pressure you with guilt. Guilt will only exacerbate the problem. Jesus came to destroy guilt in his elect, not to increase it. As Paul says,

> There is therefore now no condemnation for those who are in Christ Jesus. For the law of the Spirit of life has set you free in Christ Jesus from the law of sin and death. (Rom 8:1–2)

God wants us to admit our sin, however, just as he wanted Adam to do in the garden. We have sinned by being ashamed of the doctrine of hell. We have sinned by avoiding the issue. We have sinned by questioning God's goodness in condemning the wicked. We have sinned by not loving sinners enough to confront them with the truth. We have sinned by not loving God enough to proclaim his message faithfully. Christ is the only fount for cleansing. We cannot conquer guilt by self-effort. Only the blood of Jesus can break its power. The gospel offers a continuously cleansing fountain for any who will admit their weakness. We bring our guilt to Jesus. We who have "no money" purchase cleansing and renewal from him "without money and without price" (Isa. 55:1). The Holy Spirit is the only fount for power. We do not use guilt as a power to be better. We humble ourselves before a merciful Savior. We look to God's Spirit to sanctify our hearts. We ask for the love to speak the truth to the world.

FOR FURTHER REFLECTION

1. Read Matthew 23. Why does Jesus use such strong words in this chapter? Which of the sins listed in this chapter apply to you? Notice Jesus' desire in verse 37. Despite the sin of Israel's leaders, Jesus still desires to extend grace to them. That same grace is offered to us. Confess any hypocrisy in your life and ask for Jesus to gather you to him and to heal you.
2. In his sermon "The Method of Grace" George Whitefield asked his listeners, "Did you ever feel and experience this, any of you—to justify God in your damnation—to own that you are by nature children of wrath, and that God may justly cut you off?"[12] How would you answer?
3. Would you say that you are ashamed of the doctrine of hell? Would it embarrass you to talk with unbelievers about God's justice?

CHAPTER ELEVEN

HUMAN TRAFFICKING (3:4)

*For this perhaps is why he was parted from you for a
while, that you might have him back forever, no longer
as a bondservant but more than a bondservant, as a
beloved brother. (Philem. 15–16)*

The book *Not for Sale: The Return of the Global Slave
Trade—and How We Can Fight It* begins with the
claim that "more than 30 million slaves live in our
world today. Girls and boys, women and men of all ages
are forced to toil in the rug-loom sheds of Nepal, sell their
bodies in the brothels of Rome, break rocks in the quarries
of Pakistan, fight wars in the jungles of Africa, and sew
clothes in the garment factories of California."[1] For those
of us who are used to thinking about slavery in the context of the pre–Civil War African slave trade, this number
sounds outlandish. In other ways, David Batstone's number
errs conservatively. One could make an excellent case, for
instance, that North Korea's twenty-four million citizens
all function as slaves for the Kim dynasty. Defining slavery
proves difficult; quantifying it proves even more difficult.
The illegality of the global slave trade makes it fractured and
secretive. Available statistics are only guesses, even if they
are well-researched guesses made by knowledgeable people.

Slavery has existed throughout history, and the Bible
recounts many stories, from the enslavement of the entire

Israelite people by Pharaoh to Paul's interceding with Philemon for Onesimus's freedom. This topic enters our discussion of Nahum because of a curious word in 3:4. While the ESV says that the Assyrian prostitute "betrays" nations, I would argue that translations that use either "sells" (NASB, NKJV), "selleth" (KJV), "enslaves" (NRSV), or "enslaved" (NIV) more accurately preserve the meaning of the original Hebrew.

DEFINING *PROSTITUTE*

Biblical scholars have struggled with the characterization of Assyria in Nahum 3:4 as a prostitute who sold nations. As one scholar puts it, "The metaphor of Nineveh as a prostitute is surprisingly inappropriate: the Assyrians had conquered nations; they hardly needed to sell themselves. Nor, as conquerors, did they spend much time alluring or enchanting those they conquered."[2] I have argued throughout this book that Nahum, as a brilliant poet, knew exactly what he was doing; what scholars attribute to ignorance, carelessness, or corruption should actually be credited to intention. Much of this chapter will therefore be dedicated to demonstrating that the Assyrian Empire fitted Nahum's description precisely.[3]

In order to explain 3:4, we must address two issues: how did Nineveh qualify as a prostitute, and how did it sell nations? To answer the first question, we will look to two other women whom the Old Testament labels as prostitutes: Rahab and Jezebel. In Joshua 2, Joshua sends two spies into Jericho with instructions to gather as much information as possible about the city. As with many stories in the Old Testament that deal with sexual matters, the narrator leaves some interesting questions unanswered. The two spies immediately went "into the house of a prostitute whose name was Rahab and lodged there" (2:1). The author of Joshua makes no effort to satisfy our curiosity about why this was their first stop and place of lodging. Numerous possibilities present themselves. If we want to give the spies the benefit of the doubt, we could say that they chose a place where shady characters congregated, secrets were kept, and people were willing to engage in illicit activities for money. It proved to be a wise choice, and they gained the information that they sought. Our purpose, though, is not to query the personal morality of the spies, but to examine Rahab's house. The house belonged to a prostitute, and strangers could lodge there. It clearly functioned as a place of business. We get another crucial piece of information about the house in Joshua 2:18. As Rahab brokers her deal, the spies instruct her to "gather into your house your father and mother, your brothers, and all your father's household." This command reveals that Rahab's family did not live in Rahab's "house." We must conclude, therefore, that Rahab's house functioned as a brothel, making Rahab a madam.

We will return to Rahab shortly, but before discussing her further, let us look at the story of Jezebel. Jezebel first appears in 1 Kings 16:31, which says, "And as if it had been a light thing for [Ahab] to walk in the sins of Jeroboam the son of Nebat, he took for his wife Jezebel the daughter of Ethbaal king of the Sidonians, and went and served Baal and worshiped him." The Bible has only scorn for Jezebel. She led Israel into Baal worship. She killed God's prophets. She murdered Naboth to steal his vineyard. In the final biblical reference to her, Jesus invokes her name to condemn a woman in the church of Thyatira "who calls herself a prophetess and is teaching and seducing my servants to practice sexual immorality and to eat food sacrificed to idols" (Rev. 2:20). Jesus continues by saying,

> I gave her time to repent, but she refuses to repent of her sexual immorality. Behold, I will throw her onto a sickbed, and those who commit adultery with her I will throw into great tribulation, unless they

repent of her works, and I will strike her children dead. (2:21–23)

The Bible makes it plain that Jezebel was evil and that any who follow in her path will receive God's judgment. Nahum's characterization of the Assyrian prostitute conspicuously matches the description of Jezebel in 2 Kings 9. That chapter explains how Jehu carried out God's command to "strike down the house of Ahab your master, so that I may avenge on Jezebel the blood of my servants the prophets, and the blood of all the servants of the LORD" (v. 7). Jehu sets off at breakneck speed to fulfill this task, exciting alarm in the king's ranks. When he meets King Joram, we find the following interchange: "And when Joram saw Jehu, he said, 'Is it peace, Jehu?' He answered, 'What peace can there be, so long as the whorings and the sorceries of your mother Jezebel are so many?'" (v. 22). Nahum employed the same Hebrew words for "whorings" and "sorceries" in 3:4, although the ESV translates the latter as "charms" in Nahum: "And all for the countless whorings of the prostitute, graceful and of deadly charms [sorceries], who betrays nations with her whorings, and peoples with her charms [sorceries]."

We may deduce, therefore, that Nahum considered Nineveh to be a harlot in the tradition of Jezebel. The Bible gives no indication, however, of actual sexual immorality in the life of Jezebel. It certainly does not suggest that Jezebel sold her own body for money. It charges her with a greater crime: leading Israel into adultery with foreign gods. The Bible consistently links idolatry and adultery, as in the book of Hosea. Whereas Rahab's prostitution included running a physical brothel, Jezebel's prostitution stemmed from her running a spiritual one. Likewise, Nahum charges Nineveh with running a spiritual brothel—one that prostitutes others, rather than itself. Millennia before the international community became conscious of the evils of slavery, Nahum condemned Assyria for its multinational human-trafficking operation.

DEFINING HUMAN TRAFFICKING

In the early 1800s, William Wilberforce worked tirelessly to end the African slave trade in the British Empire. Parliament rewarded Wilberforce's efforts by passing the Slavery Abolition Act in 1833 without bloodshed. Several decades later, slavery was abolished in the United States, but at the cost of hundreds of thousands of lives.

In our more modern times, Western governments have taken further legal action to try to curb human slavery across the globe. This led to the United Nations passing the Convention against Transnational Organized Crime. This convention included a definition of human trafficking that has become the legal definition in Western nations, including the United States. The United Nations defines human trafficking as

> the recruitment, transportation, transfer, harbouring or receipt of persons, by means of the threat or use of force or other forms of coercion, of abduction, of fraud, of deception, of the abuse of power or of a position of vulnerability or of the giving or receiving of payments or benefits to achieve the consent of a person having control over another person, for the purpose of exploitation. Exploitation shall include, at a minimum, the exploitation of the prostitution of others or other forms of sexual exploitation, forced labour or services, slavery or practices similar to slavery, servitude or the removal of organs.[4]

The above definition matches Assyrian boasts. The empire functioned as one of the most efficient and egregious human-trafficking enterprises that the world has ever witnessed.

We will now compare Assyrian methods of enslavement with the UN definition and practices used by modern traffickers. Since Nahum 3:4 uses sexual imagery, our examination will focus on the modern trafficking of women for prostitution.

RECRUITMENT

Slavers do what they do for profit. They are merchants. They treat human beings as merchandise, and they follow the basic principles of commerce. They seek to buy low and sell high. They are traffickers because they obtain slaves from one locale and then move them to another. They buy in the places where humans have little value, and they sell the slaves in nations with high demand. Slavers therefore exploit societies ravaged by "poverty, unemployment, war, and political and economic instability."[5] People in such societies are more vulnerable to kidnapping or deception.[6] In some cases, people enter into a life of slavery because they see no other option.

Assyria also procured its captives through kidnapping, deception, and voluntary enslavement. The latter case requires some explanation. Padam Simkhada, who studies prostitution in Nepal, explains the difficulties that lead to women entering into sexual slavery by choice.

> It is very hard to answer the question of how many girls were actually tricked or forced into the trade or how many went into the business of their own free will, because it is not clear where the dividing line is between choice and compulsion. As O'Dea noticed, the expression "own free will" seems out of place in this context. The influence of poverty, family pressure, caste and gender discrimination has to be taken into account. Mere resignation due to lack of a viable alternative may seem a rational response. In the Nepali context, "voluntary prostitution" is often considered a paradoxical term. However, it does not serve the reality of trafficked girls to fit their cases

to a dichotomous system that only admits voluntary
or forced prostitution. There are too many forces at
work to decide.[7]

It was this type of pressure that led to King Ahaz of
Judah sending "messengers to Tiglath-pileser king of
Assyria, saying, 'I am your servant and your son. Come
up and rescue me from the hand of the king of Syria and
from the hand of the king of Israel, who are attacking me'"
(2 Kings 16:7). Judah invited Assyria. They saw Assyrian
slavery as a more "viable alternative" than trusting God to
rescue them from Syria and Israel.

Other prophets condemned Judah for such spiritual
adultery. God expected his people to trust him in all circumstances. "'In returning and rest you shall be saved;
in quietness and in trust shall be your strength.' But you
were unwilling" (Isa. 30:15). Instead, Judah turned to other
nations with other gods. That message speaks loudly from
the pages of the Old Testament. Nahum contains a different but complementary message. God will severely judge
those who took advantage of Judah's dire circumstances
in order to prostitute his people. Nahum does not speak a
general message about God's judgment of wicked nations. It
speaks specifically of the fierceness of God's covenant love
and his intention to avenge himself on rivals for his bride.

Assyria also used deceit and brutal kidnapping to trap
its victims. The Bible records an example of Assyrian diplomacy, when the Rabshakeh told besieged Jerusalemites,
"Make your peace with me and come out to me. Then each
one of you will eat of his own vine, and each one of his
own fig tree, and each one of you will drink the water of
his own cistern, until I come and take you away to a land
like your own land, a land of grain and wine, a land of
bread and vineyards, a land of olive trees and honey, that
you may live, and not die" (2 Kings 18:31–32). It must have
sounded better than perishing in an Assyrian siege, but the
Judeans could not have believed the pretended compassion.

While Assyria certainly took advantage of those who accepted vassalage, it primarily took whole peoples captive by brutal force. Again, the Bible gives an example. After Ahaz solicited Assyrian aid, "the king of Assyria listened to him. The king of Assyria marched up against Damascus and took it, carrying its people captive to Kir" (2 Kings 16:9). Claims of kidnapping on a national scale fill Assyrian royal inscriptions. For example, an inscription from Tiglath-pileser III reads, "By means of earthworks [and] battering rams, I captured the city Sarrabānu. I carried off 55,000 people, together with their possessions, his booty, his property, his goods, his wife, his sons, his daughters, and his gods."[8] This is one of hundreds of examples of Assyrian recruitment and transportation of human slaves. By calculating the total deportees listed in Neo-Assyrian inscriptions, we find a record of 4.5 million deportees. Even taking into consideration the Assyrian penchant for exaggeration, this represents a staggering human toll.[9]

We must ask why Assyria deported so many people. The usual explanation views this policy as a means of subduing the conquered nation. Empires find that conquering a nation proves easier than governing it. Every empire has sought to establish a policy that results in submission and tribute without the need for continued military intervention. Certainly Assyria saw deportation as a means of preventing future rebellion. With people removed from their land and a mixture of foreigners replacing them, the national identity fades. This was the origin of the Samaritans, and we see the effects of this policy in Ezra 4.

Those who study Assyria prove less shrewd than Nahum in this matter, however. Nahum identified the Assyrian prostitute as a merchant with a profit motive. I distrust any historian who tries to give Assyrian policy the benefit of the doubt. Surprisingly, many do. When I read the Assyrian records, I see kings who lusted after money, power, and glory; they used any and all means available to them to attain these ends. I think Nahum reached the same conclusion. Nahum 3:4 uses the word "sells" to expose Assyrian deportation as economically motivated. When Assyria detailed how many captives it had taken from a certain city, the tally of people usually came first in a list of economic assets seized, as shown by the inscription of Tiglath-pileser quoted above. These texts give reason to believe that the deportation of entire populations for economic purposes was a primary reason for conquest.

SPIRITUAL PROSTITUTION

In the years preceding Nahum's prophecy, the Assyrian Empire used deportees for two massive building ventures. First, Sennacherib changed the capital of Assyria from Dur-Sharrukin to Nineveh. He then turned Nineveh into the largest, most ostentatious, and best-defended city in the ancient Near East. Second, Esarhaddon rebuilt Babylon, which Sennacherib had brutally destroyed. These projects required massive amounts of money and labor. Both came from conquest. Nahum indicted Assyria for killing, destroying, stealing, and enslaving to gain the economic resources—money, material, and labor—needed to build.

Nahum also charged Nineveh with sexual crime. Since the prophets used the language of adultery to condemn idolatry, the link between forced worship and forced prostitution becomes apparent. Nahum, therefore, named Nineveh a cosmic pimp.[10] Like modern human traffickers, Nineveh recruited vulnerable people, transported them out of their native land, forced them to commit spiritual prostitution, punished them for any perceived disloyalty, and received payment in return. The seemingly endless supply of captives replenished the ranks of victims.[11]

So how did Nineveh prostitute her captives? By considering how the Old Testament viewed oaths and service to foreign gods, it is not difficult to answer this question. The forced loyalty oaths to Assyrian deities constituted spiritual rape in Nahum's worldview. Assyria also prostituted

Israel, Judah, and other nations in other ways. The crimes listed in Nahum's indictment include economic and sexual elements because the Assyrians used the money, materials, and slave labor of Israel, Judah, and other nations to build palaces and temples dedicated to Assyrian and Babylonian gods. In biblical studies, the most famous Assyrian inscription, by far, is Sennacherib's "bird in a cage" reference to Hezekiah, which begins,

> Moreover, (as for) Hezekiah of the land Judah, who had not submitted to my yoke, I surrounded (and) conquered forty-six of his fortified cities, fortresses, and small(er) settlements in their environs, which were without number, by having ramps trodden down and battering rams brought up, the assault of foot soldiers, sapping, breaching, and siege engines. I brought out of them 200,150 people, young (and) old, male and female, horses, mules, donkeys, camels, oxen, and sheep and goats, which were without number, and I counted (them) as booty.[12]

This excerpt comes from a much longer inscription. The first part of the inscription, which includes the encounter with Hezekiah, details five of Sennacherib's military campaigns. The second part gives extensive details of the massive expansion of Nineveh. The rebuilding account begins,

> At that time, Nineveh, the exalted cult center, the city loved by the goddess Ištar in which all of the rituals for gods and goddesses are present; the enduring foundation (and) eternal base whose plan had been designed by the stars (lit. "writing") of the firmament and whose arrangement was made manifest since time immemorial; a sophisticated place (and) site of secret lore in which every kind of skilled craftsmanship, all of the rituals, (and) the secret(s) of the *lalgar* (cosmic subterranean water) are apprehended.[13]

The inscription proceeds to provide details about the materials and engineering required to transform Nineveh in both size and luxury. Many of these buildings were dedicated to Assyrian gods and goddesses. Although it is not explicitly stated, the Assyrians certainly would have used slaves from Israel and Judah for these projects.

REDEMPTION

I spent some of my high school and college summers working as a counselor at Triple "C" Bible Camp in rural North Carolina. I learned much through this experience, including quite a few verses in King James English and many Baptist songs about Jesus' blood that were not typical fare in my Presbyterian church back home. One of the gospel songs we sang over and over began,

> I've been redeemed (I've been redeemed)
> by the blood of the Lamb. (by the blood of the Lamb.)
> I've been redeemed (I've been redeemed)
> by the blood of the Lamb,
> I've been redeemed by the blood of the Lamb,
> saved and sanctified I am.
> All my sins are washed away,
> I've been redeemed.

As I write this, the tune is running through my head. It will probably remain in my subconscious for most of the day. Some of you no doubt have the song in your head as well. Many other songs, such as Keith Green's "There Is a Redeemer,"[14] come to mind as well. It seems that the name "Redeemer Presbyterian Church" has become quite popular of late. We are right to emphasize and worship the redemptive work of Christ.

The contrast between Jesus' redemption and the Assyrian prostitute's consumption could not be starker. The

Assyrians murdered, pillaged, and kidnapped for the grat-
ification of their lusts. The spirit of Assyria remains rampant
today. The book of Revelation picked up the imagery of
Nahum 3:4 to describe "the great prostitute who is seated
on many waters, with whom the kings of the earth have
committed sexual immorality, and with the wine of whose
sexual immorality the dwellers on earth have become drunk"
(Rev. 17:1–2). John continued his description by saying,

> The woman was arrayed in purple and scarlet, and
> adorned with gold and jewels and pearls, holding
> in her hand a golden cup full of abominations and
> the impurities of her sexual immorality. And on her
> forehead was written a name of mystery: "Baby-
> lon the great, mother of prostitutes and of earth's
> abominations." And I saw the woman, drunk with
> the blood of the saints, the blood of the martyrs of
> Jesus. (Rev. 17:4–6)

The lust for power and luxury has always driven the human
slave trade.

Whereas the Assyrian prostitute, the Babylonian prostitute, and every human society have sought to consume others to satisfy endless greed, Jesus redeemed us. To redeem
is to purchase back. Hosea redeemed his wayward wife with
"fifteen shekels of silver and a homer and a lethech of barley"
(Hos. 3:2). Boaz redeemed his future wife by purchasing
"from the hand of Naomi all that belonged to Elimelech"
(Ruth 4:9). Christ redeemed us from slavery by his blood.

Our first father sold us into slavery for food. We dare
not shift blame, though, for we have continued to sell
ourselves to Satan for payment just as paltry. He offers
us trinkets, pleasures, and praise, and we gladly give him
our most precious treasures in exchange. The difference
between our spiritual slavery and the human slavery that
Not for Sale describes is twofold: we do not know that we
are slaves, and our condition is much worse.

Jesus came to redeem a people who did not want to be redeemed. The world responds to Christ as Israel responded to Moses and as Judah responded to Samson. They said, "The LORD look on you and judge, because you have made us stink in the sight of Pharaoh and his servants, and have put a sword in their hand to kill us" (Ex. 5:21). "Do you not know that the Philistines are rulers over us? What then is this that you have done to us?" (Judg. 15:11). But the reaction that Jesus received exceeded those: "They kept shouting, 'Crucify, crucify him!'" (Luke 23:21). The world has come to love and worship the prostitute. It would rather be prostituted by her than be liberated by Christ.

The book of Revelation spoke to the early church as it eased into compromise. The Holy Spirit drew back the curtain so that John could see the true condition of the world, the evil powers behind it, and the ways in which Christ's bride had begun giving herself to those powers. As the biblical canon closed, the early church stood in danger of demonic compromise. I confess that I think our state is worse than theirs. When Jesus told the church of Laodicea, "For you say, I am rich, I have prospered, and I need nothing" (Rev. 3:17), he also spoke forward to us. I hope I am wrong. I hope that you and your church have not compromised yourselves to the spirit of the age, "choosing rather to be mistreated with the people of God than to enjoy the fleeting pleasures of sin" (Heb. 11:25). If this describes you, take comfort. "The one who conquers, I will grant him to sit with me on my throne, as I also conquered and sat down with my Father on his throne" (Rev. 3:21). If, though, you recognize that you have given yourself into slavery, Jesus offers to redeem you. He will buy you out of your slavery so that you may be free to worship him. To all of us, the voice from heaven calls, "Come out of her, my people, lest you take part in her sins, lest you share in her plagues; for her sins are heaped high as heaven, and God has remembered her iniquities" (Rev. 18:4–5).

165

FOR FURTHER REFLECTION

1. Read Ephesians 6:5–9, Colossians 3:22–4:1, and Philemon. How does the global slave trade affect how you understand these passages?
2. Find a Bible passage that equates idolatry and adultery, and meditate on it. In what ways are you guilty of spiritual adultery against God?
3. In what ways does our modern culture attempt to seduce us away from God? To which of these are you most susceptible?
4. Read Ruth 4. How did Boaz redeem Ruth? How does the book of Ruth point forward to Jesus' redemption of us?
5. When Revelation 18:4–5 calls us out of our seductive culture, do you want to be delivered? Why or why not?

CHAPTER TWELVE

THE GREAT PROSTITUTE
(3:5–7)

After this I heard what seemed to be the loud voice of a
great multitude in heaven, crying out,

"Hallelujah!
Salvation and glory and power belong to our God,
for his judgments are true and just;
for he has judged the great prostitute
who corrupted the earth with her immorality,
and has avenged on her the blood of his servants."
(Rev. 19:1–2)

A few years ago, I preached through Ezekiel. I prefer
to do sermon series that work through a book of
the Bible. This method forces a preacher to address,
or at least to mention, the parts of the Bible that he would
not otherwise deal with. Ezekiel provided a number of
opportunities to talk about aspects of God's character that
have faded from prominence of late. Two particular passages, though, made me think twice about even reading
them aloud in church. Even though "all Scripture is . . .
profitable" (2 Tim. 3:16), the thought of reading the graphic
sexual language in Ezekiel 16 and 23 to a congregation
including young children did make me pause.[1] However, I
decided that it would be a grave mistake to censor Scripture

out of my own insecurity. God's Word is a "hammer that breaks the rock in pieces" (Jer. 23:29). We need all of it. We especially need the sexually graphic parts of Scripture in our age of hypersexual media saturation. God's Word rips away the erotic exterior that the world offers, showing instead the demonic horror of sexual immorality. Each of the last two chapters of the Bible says that God will consign the sexually immoral to hell (Rev. 21:8; 22:15). Our culture must wake up to this danger.

The graphic nature of Nahum 3:5-7 has attracted attention over the last twenty-five years. Over that time, a number of academic articles have argued that these verses record a rape scene.[2] The strongest words come from Judith Sanderson.

> What would it mean to worship a God who is portrayed as raping women when angry? And if humans see themselves in some way as the image of God, what would it mean to reflect that aspect of God's activity on the human level? To involve God in an image of sexual violence is, in a profound way, somehow to justify it and thereby to sanction it for human males who are for any reason angry with a woman. No wonder, then, that these biblical passages are seldom used for preaching and teaching.[3]

I disagree with Sanderson's assessment. While the context of Nineveh's fall may lead a reader to reach her conclusion, and while sexual assault and rape have a long and tragic association with war,[4] we will see that Nahum 3:7 does not allow that interpretation.

In Nahum 3:5-6, God promises Nineveh's queen that he "will lift up your skirts over your face; and I will make nations look at your nakedness and kingdoms at your shame. I will throw filth at you and treat you with contempt and make you a spectacle." We can imagine such a scene during the battle of Nineveh. After a four-month siege, the

Babylonians and Medes breached the city. Soldiers poured in. The archaeological record indicates they smashed, burned, and pillaged. We may infer from Nahum's words that the soldiers captured Nineveh's queen and brought her to a public square in order to humiliate her before the victorious soldiers and defeated citizens. Let us stop here and ask a question. If we assume that the intent was to "undress her in public so that strange men would have the opportunity to gaze with lust upon her breasts and genitals,"[5] how would you expect victorious Babylonian soldiers to respond to the sight? Hopefully I will be forgiven for prejudging these Babylonian warriors. I doubt that their character would show itself noble in this moment. However they would have reacted in this moment, such a scene is not pictured in Nahum 3:7.

I believe that the ESV understates the reaction when it reads, "And all who look at you will shrink from you" (Nah. 3:7). But we do not need to argue the Hebrew. However we translate it, God's stripping of this woman causes repulsion—not lust—in the hearts of the onlookers.

There is a better explanation for Nahum 3:5–7. These verses describe the cultic desecration of the goddess Ishtar. After God destroyed Ishtar's city, he would drag this goddess of love and war before all of her loyal subjects, remove the erotic façade, and show the world the true demonic horror that she was.

A similar event had happened earlier in biblical history. In the previous chapter, we saw the similarity between the Assyrian prostitute and Jezebel. We now have another. When Jehu came to kill Jezebel, she "painted her eyes and adorned her head" (2 Kings 9:30). Despite Jezebel's efforts, God saw to it that she lost her exterior beauty and became a revolting sight. I will let 2 Kings tell the rest of the story.

> And as Jehu entered the gate, [Jezebel] said, "Is it peace, you Zimri, murderer of your master?" And he lifted up his face to the window and said, "Who is on

my side? Who?" Two or three eunuchs looked out at him. He said, "Throw her down." So they threw her down. And some of her blood spattered on the wall and on the horses, and they trampled on her. Then he went in and ate and drank. And he said, "See now to this cursed woman and bury her, for she is a king's daughter." But when they went to bury her, they found no more of her than the skull and the feet and the palms of her hands. When they came back and told him, he said, "This is the word of the LORD, which he spoke by his servant Elijah the Tishbite, 'In the territory of Jezreel the dogs shall eat the flesh of Jezebel, and the corpse of Jezebel shall be as dung on the face of the field in the territory of Jezreel, so that no one can say, This is Jezebel.'" (2 Kings 9:31–37)

In a few hours, this queen who had exercised control over all those around her became an object of horror. Nahum 3:5–7 prophesies the same result for Nineveh's goddess.

At this point, some more background on Ishtar may help. Ishtar myths combine sex, war, and death. They depict her as powerful, seductive, and dangerous. *The Epic of Gilgamesh* contains an encounter with Ishtar that illustrates these characteristics. In tablet six, the semi-divine hero, Gilgamesh, captures Ishtar's notice as he bathes. She tries to seduce him:

Come to me, Gilgamesh, and be my lover!
Bestow on me the gift of your fruit!
You can be my husband, and I can be your wife.
I shall have a chariot of lapis lazuli and gold har-
 nessed for you,
With wheels of gold, and horns of *elmēšu*-stone.[6]

Gilgamesh spurns Ishtar's advances because he knows that misery awaits him if he complies. He asks "Which of your lovers [lasted] forever?"[7] He then recounts the miserable end of those whom Ishtar has seduced. This response sends Ishtar into a rage, and she demands that the god Anu send the Bull of Heaven to destroy Gilgamesh. Anu refuses until Ishtar threatens,

> I shall set my face towards the infernal regions,
> I shall raise up the dead, and they will eat the living.
> I shall make the dead outnumber the living![8]

Anu's acquiescence identifies Ishtar as capable, in both character and ability, of committing such a deed.

Ishtar's seduction and ruination of those who accept or rebuff her advances correspond to the Neo-Assyrian Empire's treatment of its vassals.[9] Assyria's power "was seductive for other nations. The culture of dominant nations does not need to be imposed; it is seductive by its very power."[10] Assyria actively enticed nations and proved adept at diplomacy. The empire had many opportunities for "political deals with foreign rulers (or would-be rulers) seeking military aid, peace or other favours from the Assyrian king. By signing a treaty with the Assyrian emperor, these rulers traded off their national independence for Assyrian vassalage."[11] Expansion by these means proved easier and less costly than military conquest. Ishtar represented the seductive nature of Assyria.

Ishtar imagery in Nahum 3:4–7 also explains the crowd's revulsion at the queen's exposure. Ishtar's naked body played a crucial role in her cult, as evidenced by both literature and art. In fact, Mesopotamian religion emphasized the erotic.

> Nudity or nakedness are common motifs that appear in a number of forms of representation, and descriptions of erotic aspects of nudity or undressed bodies are common in all manner of literary genres. . . . High art and what we would call 'pornography' were not differentiated genres in ancient Mesopotamia, where

visual images and literary texts that might today be described as pornographic were often pious works associated with a deity's cult.[12]

It would not be controversial to say that this aspect of Mesopotamian religion focused on the goddess Ishtar. Because of the frequency with which Ishtar's naked body was portrayed, artistically and literarily, "almost any Assyrian representation of a largely naked woman is liable to be seen as some representation of Ishtar."[13]

Mesopotamian religion ascribed supernatural power to Ishtar's body. Ishtar's naked body was, therefore, essential to her cult. In fact, "the goddess's body and her literally spellbinding sexuality were important instruments of Old Babylonian household magic,"[14] and were therefore part of what Nahum would call her "sorceries" (Nah. 3:4).

Nahum used a brilliant literary technique when he set the scene of Queen Nineveh's public exposure after the city's fall. He led us to expect sensuality and then actually produced the macabre. Unfortunately, because readers have typecast Nahum, they have not read it carefully enough to notice the surprise ending.

NAHUM AND REVELATION

Lest you charge me with imaginative hermeneutical wrangling, I have only offered the same interpretation of Nahum 3 that the New Testament gives. The similarities between the great whore in Revelation 17–18 and Queen Nineveh in Nahum 2:8; 3:4–7 are striking. The harlot that John saw met the same end as Jezebel and the Assyrian prostitute.

The waters that you saw, where the prostitute is seated, are peoples and multitudes and nations and languages. And the ten horns that you saw, they and the beast will hate the prostitute. They will make her desolate and naked, and devour her flesh and burn her up with fire, for God has put it into their hearts to carry out his purpose by being of one mind and handing over their royal power to the beast, until the words of God are fulfilled. (Rev. 17:15–17)

In 2 Kings, Nahum, and Revelation, God's judgment rips away a false, erotic exterior to reveal the true horror below. In each text, a woman has seduced and controlled God's people, causing them to commit abominations. Her outward beauty has been a means of control. In each text, God removes the erotic exterior in order to break the spell that the sorceress has cast over his beloved. In each case, his judgment achieves its goal. God does not commit rape in Nahum 3. He exercises righteous judgment so that a cosmic madam will no longer have the power to prostitute God's people.

May God do so again today. We desperately need him to deliver us from our intoxication with Babylon's charms. Revelation 18 lists her items of luxury: "gold, silver, jewels, pearls, fine linen, purple cloth, silk, scarlet cloth, all kinds of scented wood, all kinds of articles of ivory, all kinds of articles of costly wood, bronze, iron and marble, cinnamon, spice, incense, myrrh, frankincense, wine, oil, fine flour, wheat, cattle and sheep, horses and chariots, and slaves, that is, human souls" (Rev. 18:12–13). This list, so impressive in John's day, pales in comparison to the articles in any of our houses. No people in history have enjoyed as much luxury as we have. Our ancestors could not even have imagined some of the things that we take for granted. Could anyone more desperately need this warning than we do?

The last item in John's list of the harlot's consumer goods is "human souls." Our society has paid a high cost for these luxuries. Benjamin Nolot founded the ministry Exodus Cry, which works to abolish sex slavery.[15] He recently wrote, "By the time most [girls] reach adolescence they have become fully amalgamated into the culture's narrative—To be powerful, accepted, celebrated, appreciated, and adored—to be VISIBLE, you must be SEXUAL. The alternative is to be rendered completely and entirely irrelevant—to be made INVISIBLE."[16] The sexual saturation of our nation takes a terrible toll. The Song of Solomon repeatedly warns us to "not stir up or awaken love until it pleases" (Song 2:7; 3:5; 8:4). In direct violation of that command, little girls learn to dress and act sensually from the earliest ages. Little boys are constantly bombarded with sexual images, awakening desires that they do not understand and cannot handle—long before God intended. A staggering number of men drink in pornography obsessively. The list of sexual tragedies and debaucheries could go on endlessly. We live in a culture addicted to its pleasure and its luxury.

What is worse, the seductive society all around us prevents us from coming to terms with its truly horrific nature. I have heard hundreds of people thank God in their prayers that we live in a society where we have the freedom to worship God. Indeed, this is a tremendous blessing, and I in no way want to diminish that gift. I do not recall, however, ever hearing someone cry out in prayer for God to deliver him or her from the demonically seductive power of our culture. We naively assume that our souls are safer than those of our brothers and sisters in Iraq, North Korea, or Saudi Arabia. They are not. Those Christians know their weakness, and they know the danger they face. This equips them to fight day and night for the preservation of their souls. We seem to know neither, and we live on in complacency, with an occasional warning that the day may come when the police come to our home or church to take us to jail for our faith.

We face dangers far more insidious than blatant state persecution. What we desperately need—and what would be a most gracious gift from God—is that he would strip off the erotic exterior of American culture and force us to comprehend the truly horrific nature of what we have sold ourselves to. We cannot deliver ourselves. We must be delivered. It will not happen unless God does it. If you ask and beg him to, he promises to answer that prayer. I pray this for my own soul. I pray this for my family, as well, that no one in my family would be like Paul's erstwhile companion Demas: "For Demas, in love with this present world, has deserted me" (2 Tim. 4:10). I urge you to pray this as well.

In Nahum 3:5, God tells the harlot, "Behold, I am against you." Everything she stands for, everything she does, works to destroy the people of God. We see this in the famous talking-donkey story in Numbers 22–25. The king of Moab hired a spiritual hit man to curse Israel. Despite Balaam's prodigious skill in divination, he proved impotent against God's people. This led him to suggest a more effective solution. Balaam knew that God himself would curse Israel if they engaged in sexual debauchery. God killed 24,000 Israelites as a result.

Our immoral society is an abomination to God, but that is not our primary concern here. Look at what Paul said about this:

> I wrote to you in my letter not to associate with sexually immoral people—not at all meaning the sexually immoral of this world, or the greedy and swindlers, or idolaters, since then you would need to go out of the world. But now I am writing to you not to associate with anyone who bears the name of brother if he is guilty of sexual immorality or greed, or is an idolater, reviler, drunkard, or swindler—not even to eat with such a one. For what have I to do with judging outsiders? Is it not those inside the church whom you are to judge? God judges those outside. "Purge the evil person from among you." (1 Cor. 5:9–13)

Notice the distinction that Paul makes between immorality within the church and immorality without. Paul expects the pagans to be immoral. This is the logical expression of their beliefs. He makes it clear that we may associate with them. Paul's concern in this passage is with those inside the church whose behavior matches that of the culture, despite their profession of faith in Christ. Paul—the apostle of grace—commands Christians to purge the church of the sexually immoral.

Our problem comes from not understanding the absolute horror of this sin. We find the idea of Jezebel's body parts being strewn around by ravenous dogs repulsive. Yet we have grown accustomed to (perhaps addicted to?) the seductive enticements of our society that God hates, because we cannot see (or refuse to see?) the evil of them.

Most American prostitutes are essentially enslaved to pimps who use threats, beatings, drugs, and terror to force them into—and keep them in—a lifestyle that they hate and cannot escape from. A significant percentage of prostitutes worldwide have been kidnapped and tortured into submission. These are the same women appearing on the computer screens of our unattended children. They portray a happy, seductive image because they will be beaten if they do not. The sexual immorality of our society destroys the souls of little boys and little girls. It destroys the souls of grown men and grown women. It destroys families and kills by disease. The cost of all this is "human souls" (Rev. 18:13), and God hates it. God knows the horror of it. Pray that you would understand it as well.

It is likely that some of you reading this book are addicted to pornography. Perhaps some of you are now in an adulterous relationship or are practicing homosexuality. Some of you may be involved in premarital promiscuity. I have done enough counseling to know that if you are sexually addicted and are reading a book on Nahum, you have probably confessed, repented, and tried to change hundreds of times. You likely now live in resignation that nothing will change.

If the above paragraph describes you, I would like to give you two points of counsel. First, Romans 1:24–28 teaches that sexual addiction is a judgment from God. For-give me for sounding harsh. Romans 1:24 says, "God gave them up in the lusts of their hearts to impurity." This is important, because sexual immorality is not the root prob-lem. To be set free, you must address the root problem. Fortunately, Romans also tells us the reason that God gives someone over to these horrors. If you follow the logical progression in Romans 1, you will find that the outward manifestations of Romans 1:24–28 arise because people "knew God" but "did not honor him as God or give thanks to him" (v. 21). According to this verse, sexual immorality is a judgment for a specific sin: failing to worship and thank God sincerely. The road to cleansing begins with praise and thanks—not superficially mouthing empty words and meaningless phrases. God desires you to thank him for all things. If you find yourself able to do this, it will begin to break the power of this sin in your life.

Second, the Westminster Confession of Faith offers excellent teaching on this subject in the chapter on assur-ance (WCF 18). I encourage you to look this up and med-itate on it. As mentioned before, Revelation says that the sexually immoral will not enter heaven. "But as for the cowardly, the faithless, the detestable, as for murderers, the sexually immoral, sorcerers, idolaters, and all liars, their portion will be in the lake that burns with fire and sulfur, which is the second death" (Rev. 21:8). If you are caught in this sin, you must consider the possibility that you have never truly been converted. I am not saying that you have not been. I am saying that your lifestyle should make you question this deeply. It is at this point that the Confession proves so helpful. In 18.1, it says, "hypocrites and other unregenerate men may vainly deceive themselves with false hopes and carnal presumptions of being in the favour of God." On the other hand, 18.4 offers this counsel: "True believers may have the assurance of their salvation divers ways shaken, diminished, and intermitted; as, by negli-gence in preserving of it; by falling into some special sin,

which woundeth the conscience and grieveth the Spirit."
This chapter does a magnificent job explaining two difficult
subjects. Hypocrites often have a false assurance. Believers
may not have assurance. If you are caught in sexual sin,
you should question your faith. You should evaluate your
faith on a biblical basis rather than on a man-made one.
The Confession states that the biblical basis for assurance is

> the divine truth of the promises of salvation, the
> inward evidence of those graces unto which these
> promises are made, the testimony of the Spirit of
> adoption witnessing with our spirits that we are the
> children of God, which Spirit is the earnest of our
> inheritance, whereby we are sealed to the day of
> redemption. (WCF 18.2)

A thorough, biblical examination of your soul can only
help. Sexual sin will cause you to question your salvation, if
only subconsciously. By addressing the issue head-on, you
will bring this struggle into light. If you find through this
that you do truly belong to Christ, it will bring comfort to
your struggle. If you find that you are not truly converted,
this also gives great hope. You have all the promises of
Scripture that "whoever comes to me I will never cast out."
The sin you are living in results from your nature. You have
tried to conquer it with your own efforts. Humble yourself
before God and struggle with him until he answers.

The Bible commands us to "work out your own salvation
with fear and trembling" (Phil. 2:12). Likewise, "But from
there you will seek the LORD your God and you will find him,
if you search after him with all your heart and with all your
soul" (Deut. 4:29). Our spiritual ancestors knew this. It used
to be known that a man "may wait long, and conflict with
many difficulties, before he be partaker of it" (WCF 18.3).

If you have never wrestled with God until you have
found this assurance from the Holy Spirit, you must begin
today. Bunyan's *Pilgrim's Progress* provides an excellent

example of this experience. As Christian and Hopeful take their pilgrimage, Christian asks Hopeful how he came to salvation. Hopeful recounts how Faithful spoke to him about his sin and need for Christ. Hopeful explains,

> I told him that I knew not what to say when I came; and he bid say to this effect: God be merciful to me a sinner, and make me to know and believe in Jesus Christ; for I see, that if his righteousness had not been, or I have not faith in that righteousness, I am utterly cast away. Lord, I have heard that thou art a merciful God, and hast ordained that thy Son Jesus Christ should be the Saviour of the world; and moreover, that thou art willing to bestow him upon such a poor sinner as I am (and I am a sinner indeed), Lord, take therefore this opportunity, and magnify thy grace in the salvation of my soul, through thy Son Jesus Christ. Amen.

Christian: And did you do as you were bidden?

Hopeful: Yes; over, and over, and over.

Christian: And did the Father reveal the Son to you?

Hopeful: Not at the first, nor second, nor third, nor fourth, nor fifth, no, nor at the sixth time neither.

Christian: What did you do then?

Hopeful: What! why I could not tell what to do.

Christian: Had you not thoughts of leaving off praying?

Hopeful: Yes; an hundred times, twice told.

Christian: And what was the reason you did not?

179

Hopeful: I believed that it was true which hath been told me, to wit, That without the righteousness of this Christ, all the world could not save me; and therefore, thought I with myself, If I leave off, I die, and I can but die at the throne of grace. And withal, this came into my mind, 'If it tarry, wait for it; because it will surely come, and will not tarry.' So I continued praying until the Father showed me his Son.[17]

In this prayer—as in all prayer according to his will—God will answer the persistent and humble suppliant.

FOR FURTHER REFLECTION

1. Do you find the thought of sexual sin attractive or abhorrent? This question reveals your appetites. Your soul hungers for food, and it has become accustomed to righteousness or to unrighteousness. If you desire unrighteousness, pray that God would open your eyes to the realities of what you have desired.
2. Do you think of our culture as dangerous to your faith? If you have children, do you worry about our society destroying their souls? Although Satan uses different tactics in the West than he does elsewhere in the world, we are in no less peril. Pray for God to safeguard you.
3. Read chapter 18 of the Westminster Confession of Faith. Do you have a biblical assurance of salvation, based on the criteria listed in the chapter?
4. How is Jesus' perfect sexuality good news for us as broken people?

CHAPTER THIRTEEN

NO CONFIDENCE IN THE FLESH (3:8-10)

For we are the circumcision, who worship by the Spirit
of God and glory in Christ Jesus and put no confidence
in the flesh. (Phil. 3:3)

In January 1991, I was a freshman at the University of North Carolina. One night, as I walked with friends to the basketball arena to watch a game against North Carolina State, I was puzzled to see crowds of people walking toward me. When asked about the abnormal traffic pattern, they replied that the game had been cancelled. President Bush had authorized air strikes against Iraq, and Operation Desert Shield had become Operation Desert Storm. We went back to the dorms and watched the news, and a somber mood settled over the campus.

Living in the dorm room next to mine were three Reserve Officer Training Corp (ROTC) students. I had classes with students who were reservists in the Armed Forces or National Guard. Their thoughts turned to what this war might mean for them. Before then, their commitments had seemed to provide training and financial assistance for their education with little risk of having to go to war. Now the implications of the contracts they had signed became more apparent. As it turned out, few of these students would see military duty during the First Gulf War. Many of us, though, do know soldiers who went to Saudi Arabia in 1990–1991. That helps us to understand the Assyrian invasion of Thebes mentioned in Nahum 3:8–10. For Nahum's first readers, that had happened in recent memory—about twenty-five years before. As in the case of my friends at UNC, a contract had obligated Judean soldiers to go to war if Assyria decided to mobilize them. Also, Nahum's readers would have known family, friends, or neighbors who participated in that war. This helps us to understand three seemingly confusing verses.

Nahum's section on Thebes begins with a blunt question addressed to the Assyrian prostitute: "Are you better than Thebes?" This rhetorical question humbles the harlot by showing her to be inferior to a better woman in at least six ways. We will now compare the two cities on the basis of their deities, beauty, fortifications, allies, age, and empires.

DEITIES

Nahum refers to Thebes as "No-Amon," meaning "city of Amon." Some English translations of the Bible, such as the NASB and the NKJV, retain the phrase "No-Amon," rather than using the more familiar name Thebes. By labeling Thebes in this way, Nahum draws attention to its relationship with the Egyptian god Amun.[1] In this way, Nahum contrasts the city dedicated to Mesopotamia's petulant goddess of love and war with the Egyptian city devoted to their creator god. If Egypt's most powerful god could not protect his capital city, Nineveh should have no expectation that Ishtar would hold back the true God of the universe.

BEAUTY

Nahum also makes a direct attack on the beauty of Ishtar and Nineveh. English versions properly translate the first words of 3:8 as "Are you better than Thebes?" but the Hebrew also includes the question, "Are you more beautiful than Thebes?" The words that the ESV translates as "graceful" in 3:4 and "better" in 3:8 are adjectival and verbal forms of a Hebrew word that also pertains to beauty. In the context of 3:4, it is clear that personified Nineveh relies on her beauty to seduce and control others. Nahum likewise personifies Thebes as a woman and asks Nineveh a pointed question: "Who is more attractive?"

While Nineveh gloried in its art and architecture, the grandeur and beauty of Thebes dwarfed Nineveh's splendor in every regard. Ninevite artists specialized in depicting atrocity. Theban artists and architects, on the other hand, spent roughly a millennium producing immense structures whose ruins still inspire awe in modern visitors. Nineveh enjoyed a brief ascendancy in which colossal palaces arose, but these were decorated with stone reliefs of grotesque scenes. Nineveh's art focused on evoking fear and horror. Whereas Nineveh enjoyed prosperity for less than a century, Pharaohs had created architectural marvels in Thebes since before the time of the exodus. Fabulous wealth, quickly gained and extravagantly spent, does not always make for artistic beauty.

Empires create art to glorify themselves and impress others. The edifices of Nineveh and Thebes both projected power and grandeur. They sent powerful visual messages to visiting dignitaries. Nahum warned Nineveh that if Theban beauty could not cow, pacify, or seduce potential aggressors, Nineveh's beauty would be no help either.

FORTIFICATIONS

The remainder of Nahum 3:8 describes Thebes's natural defenses. With characteristic repetition, Nahum makes four references to water barriers in just a handful of words. This description of Thebes sitting "by the Nile, with water around her, her rampart a sea, and water her wall" has caused numerous scholars to question Nahum's knowledge of the city and therefore the accuracy of the Bible. Some have argued that this description of the city's water differs so drastically with Theban geography that Nahum's "No-Amon" could not be Thebes at all. Currently, most scholars acknowledge that the book does refer to Thebes, even if Nahum had faulty information. After all, how could we expect a seventh-century B.c. Judean to give an accurate description of a faraway Egyptian city?

Ultimately, we do not know how Nahum knew what he knew. He seems intimately acquainted with Assyrian texts. Had Nahum been to Nineveh as part of a diplomatic delegation? Was Assyrian propaganda so prevalent that even children knew these details? We do not know. The Theban geography question is not difficult, however. Judah had sworn to serve the Assyrian king loyally in all that he asked. Assyria had called up Judean troops for their Egyptian campaigns. Judean soldiers and citizens came back to tell the stories. In an oral culture, these events would have been told and retold. Nahum and his audience knew that Thebes was not an island kingdom, surrounded by seas and moats. We may read 3:8 and picture that, but Nahum's first readers would not have made that mistake.

What many scholars fail to recognize is that Nahum describes the water defenses on a greater scale. Thebes was not powerfully defended by water at its front door. It was powerfully defended by water at its coasts. Let's bring this home a bit. I live in West Virginia, on the border with Ohio and Kentucky. During World War II, the U.S. government built chemical and munitions plants here. One nearby town bears the name Nitro because of this. A system of rivers and railroads made this a strategic location for manufacturing and shipping munitions. During World War II, neither the Germans nor the Japanese invaded Nitro. They did not even bomb it, even though it produced war material. It was not the Kanawha River that protected Nitro. The Atlantic and Pacific Oceans did. Whereas British munitions plants suffered through numerous Luftwaffe bombing raids, West Virginia escaped unscathed. Similarly, it was not Thebes's local water resources that made it seemingly impervious to attack. It was the combination of two brutal deserts, two seas, and the world's longest river that protected Thebes. It is these waters to which Nahum refers.

The city of Thebes did sit on the Nile—five hundred miles upstream. Beyond this, Thebes had the protection of the Mediterranean Sea to the north and the Red Sea to the east. On either side of the fertile river basin, treacherous deserts provided additional barriers. The Assyrian army, with its Judean conscripts, faced an arduous journey to Thebes. All of the geography worked to aid the Egyptians and expose the Assyrians. Despite all these advantages, Thebes fell.

By contrast, Nineveh had geographical weaknesses. The city lay in the Mesopotamian plain, easily accessible from many directions and surrounded by hostile nations. Nineveh did have some natural fortifications. It also boasted huge walls and an immense armory, but if a nation had found itself strong enough to march on Assyria, it would only have faced a fraction of the hazards that a trip to Thebes involved. Nineveh did not need to worry about this, though. Assyrian armies had subdued all the surrounding nations. No nation seemed capable of marching against the Assyrian homeland, let alone Nineveh. The day would come, however, when Assyria's armies would falter. When that day came, Nineveh would be much more vulnerable than Thebes had been.

ALLIES AND EMPIRES

Nahum 3:9 lists four peoples that Thebes had counted as allies. The prodigious natural defenses of the city were supplemented by supporting nations. Yet again, Nineveh could not compare. Assyria had no friends. No one was truly loyal. Assyria conquered and governed by fear. Peoples were starved or tortured into submission. Assyria could count on only hatred and retribution from surrounding peoples. As soon as Assyrian might weakened, they would all turn against the empire. The four allies listed in 3:9 make a more subtle point, too. Nahum shaped this verse to mimic Genesis 10:6. Let's compare these two verses.

> The sons of Ham: Cush, Egypt, Put, and Canaan. (Gen. 10:6)

> Cush was her strength;
> Egypt too, and that without limit;
> Put and the Libyans were her helpers. (Nah. 3:9)

Both verses use the names of Cush, Egypt, and Put in the same order. In Genesis they refer to patriarchs, and in Nahum they refer to peoples descended from the patriarchs. As we have seen before, Nahum understood the conflict between God and the Assyrian adversaries as an ancient one. Therefore, the question "Are you better than Thebes?" also contrasts the lineage of Thebes and Nineveh. Ancient genealogies demonstrated the hierarchy of families. In this way, Nahum compared Nineveh and Thebes with regard to their empires. The Egyptian Empire had a more continuous and glorious history than Assyria did. Within the history of the Assyrian Empire, Nineveh was of little importance until its last one hundred years. Thebes had been the city of Pharaohs for centuries. Thebes had a much higher aristocratic pedigree than Nineveh.

By comparing Nineveh and Thebes in regard to deities, beauty, fortifications, allies, age, and empires, Nahum demonstrated that Nineveh had no grounds for pride or security in comparison with Thebes. If Thebes could fall, Nineveh should fear. Nineveh's brief ascendancy depended upon God's use for it. It would crumble at his behest as well. The city had no attribute that could protect it from devastation; the recent history of Thebes had shown this.

ASSYRIAN CRIMES REMEMBERED

Nahum 3:8–10 condemns Assyria for its crimes against the people of Thebes. These verses recall the opening two chapters of Amos, which pass sentence on various peoples for similar crimes. For instance,

> For three transgressions of the Ammonites,
>   and for four, I will not revoke the punishment,
> because they have ripped open pregnant women in
>   Gilead,
>   that they might enlarge their border.
> So I will kindle a fire in the wall of Rabbah,
>   and it shall devour her strongholds,
> with shouting on the day of battle,
>   with a tempest in the day of the whirlwind;
> and their king shall go into exile,
>   he and his princes together. (Amos 1:13–15)

The passage from Amos shows that God will judge acts of cruelty committed against others. Nahum says that Assyria will receive a fate similar to that of Thebes, partly because of the atrocities committed in Thebes.

TWO GREAT MEN

The apostle Paul declares, "If anyone else thinks he has reason for confidence in the flesh, I have more" (Phil. 3:4). He then proceeds to list his Jewish pedigree. Nahum similarly challenges Nineveh's confidence in the flesh by demonstrating that a city with much more reason for confidence has been brutally desecrated. Nahum ends his section on

Thebes by describing the fate of its great men. The noblest men in the noblest city met an ignoble end. They became prizes in games of chance and left the city chained and on display. If they survived the torturous journey back to Assyria, they faced a demeaning life of slavery, doing the will of their new masters.

The rest of this chapter will focus on the contrasting lives of two such great men in the New Testament. First, we will consider the life of the rich young ruler. The Holy Spirit caused this story to be recorded three times (Matt. 19:16–22; Mark 10:17–22; Luke 18:18–23) to emphasize its importance. Here is how Luke tells the story:

> And a ruler asked him, "Good Teacher, what must I do to inherit eternal life?" And Jesus said to him, "Why do you call me good? No one is good except God alone. You know the commandments: 'Do not commit adultery, Do not murder, Do not steal, Do not bear false witness, Honor your father and mother.'" And he said, "All these I have kept from my youth." When Jesus heard this, he said to him, "One thing you still lack. Sell all that you have and distribute to the poor, and you will have treasure in heaven; and come, follow me." But when he heard these things, he became very sad, for he was extremely rich. (Luke 18:18–23)

This man possessed reputation, title, and wealth. He also longed for what theologians call assurance of salvation. The Bible grants that he desired Christ and heaven. The Bible indicates that he had lived a moral life. Jesus, who knew the thoughts of those who spoke to him (Luke 6:8), did not challenge the young man's claim to moral righteousness, as he did with the Pharisees (Matt. 23:27) or the woman at the well (John 4:17–18). Apparently, the ruler could say with Paul that he was "as to righteousness under the law, blameless" (Phil. 3:6).

How does the rich young ruler relate to Nahum? Well, Nahum begins with a declaration of God's coming wrath. He states that God will be a refuge to those who trust in him (1:7) but that the ungodly will be swept away in the flood of God's judgment (1:8). The prophet Jonah had warned Nineveh of this roughly a hundred years beforehand, and Nineveh had repented. God had relented then, but with Nahum the wrath will not turn back. In three verses (3:8–10), Nahum demolishes any hope that Nineveh can stand against God's wrath by its own power. A similar city, but superior in every way, has fallen. Now Nineveh's turn will come. The great men of Thebes were humiliated. The great men of Nineveh will meet the same end.

Almost seven hundred years later, a great man of Judah came to Jesus with the same fear. How could he escape God's coming wrath? He had every earthly advantage: power, respect, wealth, youth, and morality. But he left without the assurance he craved. None of this could protect him from God's wrath. None of these things would impress God.

Now, I want to ask a painful question. I ask you to provide an honest answer. Have you ever witnessed a church turn the rich young ruler away? Do you know a minister who would answer him in the way that Jesus did? I want to be careful here. I do not think that the problem was money. Jesus demanded that his followers switch their allegiance from this world to him. He asks different things from each of us as a demonstration that we have done that. By telling the man to sell his possessions, Jesus was forcing him to perform a visible sign of his transformation. Had he sold his possessions to follow an itinerant teacher, he would have created a scandal. He would have lost the favor of his family and of the political and religious establishments. Losing one's honor in the eyes of the world often proves more daunting than the physical sacrifices.

I offer the example of Peter as evidence. Luke 22:33–34 records the following interchange:

Peter said to him, "Lord, I am ready to go with you both to prison and to death." Jesus said, "I tell you, Peter, the rooster will not crow this day, until you deny three times that you know me."

Peter proved true to his word. When soldiers came for Jesus, Peter drew his sword "and struck the high priest's servant and cut off his right ear" (John 18:10). I submit that Peter expected this to be his last action on earth. Perhaps he thought Jesus would perform a Samson-like miracle, but Peter knew Jesus and his band to be militarily outmatched. By taking up arms in the face of superior force, Peter demonstrated his willingness to die with and for Jesus. What Peter had not counted on was the means of Jesus' death. Peter could die an honorable death on the field of battle. But he was not ready to die a shameful death—naked on a Roman cross, ridiculed by man (Mark 15:29) and cursed by God (Gal. 3:13).

This remains true today. I have known many men who have entered dangerous professions, knowing that to some degree they risked their lives every day. I have known many parents who have supported these decisions, proud that their children would devote themselves in this way. Though I have worked in churches for many years, I know few who have chosen to risk their lives in this way for the cause of Christ. Of the few that have, rarely have their parents supported this decision. The question is not the risk. Parents are proud if their sons join the Navy SEALs. The question is whether the perceived honor makes up for the risk. If society deems a path honorable, many will volunteer. NFL players know that their career choice will likely shorten their lives.[2] Similarly, people will risk death to climb Mount Everest (as the disasters in 2014 and 2015 have shown) for the glory of scaling earth's highest summit. Since society honors these accomplishments, people proceed.

Let us return then to the rich young ruler on the doorstep of your church. He desires salvation. He is willing to give and to work. He wants to know what he must do. What do we tell him? We ask if he knows that he is a sinner. He says yes. We ask if he believes that Jesus died on the cross. He says yes. We ask if he is willing to ask Jesus into his heart so that his sins can be forgiven. He says yes. We pray together. He and his family join the church. They join a small group. He gives generously. We make use of his talent and put him on a committee. We teach him and train him. After a while, he leads a Bible study, teaches Sunday school, and then becomes an elder. He dies, and the preacher talks about what a wonderful Christian man the world has lost. According to Jesus, he goes to hell. Jesus loved the rich young ruler and therefore sent him away without assurance (Mark 10:21). Do we have the courage to show the same love? Jesus also knew that this man was no asset. He would do anything necessary to gain assurance of salvation, short of losing his honor in the eyes of the world. Jesus said that the willingness to lose one's honor is the bare minimum: "Whoever does not take his cross and follow me is not worthy of me" (Matt. 10:38).

Rich young rulers go looking for a spiritual authority figure who will give them assurance of salvation. We give this assurance. They give their work and their money. This transaction is an abomination in the sight of God. The rich men of Thebes faced a judgment day at the end of Assyrian spears. Their wealth and position marked them out for greater judgment at the hands of Assyrian slave traders. The Judean ruler made a decision that he would rather have the fading honor of men than the honor of suffering scorn for Christ. He has been dead for almost two thousand years, facing the consequences of this decision.

Despite the plentiful warnings to the contrary, we still tend to consider wealth, position, and morality as effective protections against God's judgment. As Nahum 1:7 says—and so many other Scriptures as well—our accomplishments in this world are of no account in God's eyes. Only those who come broken and humbled to Christ will receive mercy and grace on that day. We cannot receive this shelter if we are unwilling to let go of our honor and reputation in this world. The world hates God (John 15:18–19) because the prince of this world hates him (John 16:11). If we are ashamed to face disgrace for Christ, and if we therefore disown him, he will disown us (Matt. 10:33).

We turn now to our second New Testament ruler who found himself in the position of the Theban nobles—who lost his rank and became helpless before the wrath of God: Jesus. I doubt that Nahum had any idea that he prophesied the fate of the coming Messiah, though perhaps he knew. In just a few words, Nahum 3:10 foretells the suffering that began and ended Jesus' life. Sometime shortly after Jesus' birth, "infants were dashed in pieces at the head of every street" as Herod's lust for power obliterated the babies of Bethlehem. The Assyrians, controlled by the same demonic power as Herod, had brutally murdered the children of Thebes.

Despite Satan's ability to rule this world and control the hearts of evil men, he had no power to touch God's Christ—until the moment set by God in which Jesus would lay down his own life (John 10:17). Then Jesus would fulfill the rest of Nahum 3:10. Unlike the "honored men" of Thebes, Jesus left his life of privilege voluntarily. Unlike the "great men" of Thebes, Jesus willfully gave himself to be "bound" by evil men. Jesus too would be paraded as a war captive, but he chose dishonor "for the joy that was set before him" (Heb. 12:2). He had much more honor and much more wealth to sacrifice than the rich young ruler did. He endured not only the scorn of his human family (Mark 3:21) but also the condemnation of his Father and God.

We stand condemned for the same sins as Nineveh, by the same God who judged Nineveh. The sentence passed against Nineveh also falls upon us. The wrath of God comes. Nothing in our flesh can stand against it. But someone came who voluntarily took this condemnation. Have the wisdom to see that all that you boast in, all that you have looked to for honor in the eyes of men, is but filth. Cast it away. Do not wait. Say, with Paul,

> Indeed, I count everything as loss because of the surpassing worth of knowing Christ Jesus my Lord. For his sake I have suffered the loss of all things and count them as rubbish, in order that I may gain Christ and be found in him, not having a righteousness of my own that comes from the law, but that which comes through faith in Christ, the righteousness from God that depends on faith—that I may know him and the power of his resurrection, and may share his sufferings, becoming like him in his death, that by any means possible I may attain the resurrection from the dead. (Phil. 3:8–11)

Throw away all that would hinder you from knowing Christ. Embrace the suffering and scorn that will come with truly following Jesus, so that you may "press on toward the goal for the prize of the upward call of God in Christ Jesus" (Phil. 3:14).

FOR FURTHER REFLECTION

1. Find an Old Testament story about Israel trusting in its own strength rather than in God (there are lots to choose from). Why did they not trust in God?
2. Find an Old Testament story about a foreign nation that defied God on the basis of its perceived strength. How patiently did God wait? How did things turn out?
3. Find a story in the Gospels in which Jesus waited upon God and depended upon the Holy Spirit. How does this story contrast with the others?
4. Read Philippians 3:1–14. To what assets or accomplishments have you looked for security? Which of

these have you learned to count as loss for the sake of Christ? Which of these do you still hold on to? Do you know what it means to have a righteousness that comes only from God? Do you desire to share in Christ's sufferings and become like him in his death?

CHAPTER FOURTEEN

THE LIBERATION OF NINEVEH (3:11–17)

The Spirit of the Lord is upon me,
because he has anointed me
to proclaim good news to the poor.
He has sent me to proclaim liberty to the captives
and recovering of sight to the blind,
to set at liberty those who are oppressed,
to proclaim the year of the Lord's favor.
(Luke 4:18–19)

On the day of his twentieth wedding anniversary, Arpád Bella faced a difficult decision. He wanted to get home to his wife. Instead, he had moments to make a decision that would alter history. Thousands of East German citizens had come to Hungary and were refusing to go home. Now, about a hundred of these refuges approached Lieutenant Colonel Bella with the intent of passing through a wooden gate into Austria. "It took him 10 seconds . . . to reach his decision: 'I don't want to be a mass murderer.' He issued the following orders to his team of four border guards: 'Face Austria and check passports if anyone comes from that direction. We don't see what happens behind us.'"[1] Bella's decision not to act opened a tear in the Iron Curtain that would never mend.

To what extent the Hungarian government originally intended to crush or encourage this breach remains unknown. Whatever the government intended, Bella's decision to ignore protocol led to thousands upon thousands of East Germans travelling to Hungary in order to cross into Austria and then find asylum in West Germany. The Hungarian government did not act to prevent the exodus. What is more, the Soviet Union did not intervene either. Eighty-two days after Bella turned his back, the Berlin wall fell.

Millions around the world watched the newscasts as citizens from both sides dismantled the concrete wall. The Soviet military, the national governments, and the secret police forces across the Eastern Europe communist bloc did nothing as one militaristic dictatorship after another fell with very little bloodshed.

The events and images of 1989 will help us to understand the final nine verses of Nahum. But before we look into this further, we must address a misconception about the book of Nahum. Commentaries on Nahum will often include a semi-apology at the outset. The authors will explain that the book has only one main theme, that God will judge the wicked nations. Nonetheless, they say, the book of Nahum is worth reading and does merit a commentary because Nahum makes his one point so well. For example, "The book of Nahum runs the risk of being monotonous because of the singularity of the author's purpose and theme. He is intent on saying only one thing: Nineveh shall fall. But the variety of methods which he employs in saying this one thing are quite remarkable and lend great force to his message."[2] In my opinion, such statements miss the tremendous depth of Nahum; they flatten a complex book and condemn it to redundancy. Why take the time to wrestle through Nahum when so many other biblical books also tell us that God judges evil? Why preach on Nahum when the same themes present themselves in books like Isaiah and Jeremiah? Why would a pastor ever dedicate a series of sermons to Nahum, only to make his congregation listen to him repeat week after week that God will judge the wicked nations? This misconception has led to Nahum's neglect. It has also caused readers to miss what the words actually say.

WHO DOES NAHUM CONDEMN?

In Nahum 1:9–15, we were introduced to the main characters of the book. In those six verses we encountered God, his prophet, the masculine plural group, an unnamed female adversary, her messenger, an unnamed male adversary, and Judah. The Belial messenger and Judah never appear outside of this passage. The remainder of the book of Nahum deals with God's judgment against "them," "her," and "him." The group of males withers at God's pronouncement. Besides the statement that "the sword shall devour your young lions" (Nah. 2:13), the prophecy decrees only a gradual decay for this group.

This leaves two characters. Of all God's enemies, the female one receives the most attention from the prophet. The male enemy gets pride of place, however, as Nahum reserves the final two verses for his demise. If we pay careful attention, we find a more limited judgment than many works on Nahum would lead us to believe.

We are told that "one must wrestle with the image of God presented in [Nahum]. A jealous, powerful, and violent deity is not one to whom many Christians wish to cling."[3] I disagree. I think there is great comfort in knowing about God's jealous love for his people. I think those who know Christ want a powerful God, not one who wrings his hands at the injustice in the world. I think preachers who dare to preach on God's wrath will find that it reassures Christ's elect. I also think that the violence in Nahum remains misunderstood because we have prejudged the book.

Let us now review. In Nahum 1:1–8, we find an angry God who rises to avenge himself on his enemies, yet those who look for refuge in him will find it. These verses do not spell out how God will avenge himself. In 1:9–15, God incapacitates evil rulers so that they may not march to war anymore. He promises to set Judah free from bondage, and he announces the end of an evil line, an evil religion, and an evil city. In 2:1–5, Nineveh comes under attack, but no specific violence is mentioned. In 2:6–10, Nineveh's defenses dissolve, her queen is carried away, and her stolen wealth is removed. The common people react strongly, but more on that later. In 2:11–13, God puts an end to Assyria's ability to kill and consume wantonly. In 3:1–3, we hear about the endless piles of corpses collected to feed the harlot's lust. In 3:4–7, God exposes the harlot for what she is, rather than what she pretends to be. He breaks her spell, and people flee. In 3:8–10, God condemns Assyria for its brutal treatment of Thebes and declares that its evil queen will fare no better.

Now let me stop here and ask a question that I have never found in any of the works on Nahum that I have read: what about this should make us uncomfortable? What part of Nahum describes an action by God that deserves anything other than thanks and worship? Nahum describes violence that the Assyrians have committed and condemns them for it. Nahum judges a select few for their actions. In some cases they just wither away. Others find harsher treatment. All of God's actions serve to put an end to violent injustice. Why should this book make us squirm? If we know God, it should not. God merely does in Nahum what he promises to do in almost every book of the Bible—hold us accountable for our sin if we do not humble ourselves before Christ, and intervene to deliver us if we do. How is Nahum any more difficult than the Sermon on the Mount, where Jesus says, "If your right hand causes you to sin, cut it off and throw it away. For it is better that you lose one of your members than that your whole body go into hell" (Matt. 5:30), and "Every tree that does not bear good fruit is cut down and thrown into the fire" (Matt. 7:19)? Why do we love the Sermon on the Mount and despise Nahum? Is the hellfire of Matthew 5 and 7 any less severe than the sword of Nahum 2:13?

God does not need to apologize to us for his vengeance. We do not need to apologize to others for him. I have no desire to find creative ways to explain away difficult Bible passages. We do not sit in judgment of Scripture; it sits in judgment of us. On the other hand, I do desire to correct what I consider to be a faulty interpretation of Nahum.

NAHUM AND THE COMMON NINEVITE

We will now examine Nahum 3:11–19 and look back to 2:6–10 to ask two specific questions. First, how did God treat the common Ninevite? Second, how did the common Ninevite respond to the city's fall? My answers to both questions will contradict accepted views. Let me provide two examples of the standard answer to these questions. Both examples come from conservative commentaries. "There is little charity in Nahum's words, little love for the citizens of Nineveh or concern for their fate. In this sense, it contrasts sharply with the book of Jonah, in which a quite different attitude towards Nineveh is expressed (and which may be read alongside Nahum as a counter-balance)."[4] Similarly, "God himself decreed the destruction of Assyria. He would make their grave. The whole people would be killed and buried together because they were 'vile.'"[5] As we will see, neither of these statements will stand when scrutinized.

When we find ordinary Assyrians in Nahum, who are they? Well, we have the slave girls in 2:7. Then we have to wait until 3:13 to find common people or "troops" mentioned. We finally get a concentration of Assyrians in 3:16–18, where "merchants," "princes," "scribes," "shepherds," "nobles," and "people" appear. So Nahum provides eight references to humans that range from general to specific and from slave to aristocrat. Does the text support the idea that "the whole people would be killed"? I confess that I do not see it. They seem scared. The slave girls are making a lot of noise, at least (we will come back to this). Well, not everyone is scared; maybe just the slave girls and the troops are scared. Like Jonah, the shepherds and nobles managed to sleep through the danger. The merchants figured things out and left. The princes and scribes did too. The "people" of 3:18 seem to have become aimless. Where exactly does God's violence come down on them?

Again, I have no interest in explaining away God's wrath. The invasion of Nineveh pictured in the book of Nahum targets specific enemies of God, yet the citizens escape unharmed. Other biblical passages show God's judgment against whole populations; Nahum does not. Let us compare Nahum with these texts to make the point.

> Now therefore, kill every male among the little ones, and kill every woman who has known man by lying with him. (Num. 31:17)

> When the LORD your God brings you into the land that you are entering to take possession of it, and clears away many nations before you, the Hittites, the Girgashites, the Amorites, the Canaanites, the Perizzites, the Hivites, and the Jebusites, seven nations more numerous and mightier than you, and when the LORD your God gives them over to you, and you defeat them, then you must devote them to complete destruction. You shall make no covenant with them and show no mercy to them. (Deut. 7:1–2)

> Now go and strike Amalek and devote to destruction all that they have. Do not spare them, but kill both man and woman, child and infant, ox and sheep, camel and donkey. (1 Sam. 15:3)

Do you see the difference? God has decreed the total destruction of a people before. He does not in Nahum. Why? I will answer that in a minute.

Before going further, I would like to show God's grace to the Assyrians through a contrast with Assyrian behavior. When Assyrian kings recorded their deeds, they emphasized the magnificence of their accomplishments. Their major victories were amazing feats, and the inconclusive battles were only slightly less amazing feats. We can read between the lines, however, by noting how many enemy soldiers died. In a great victory, Assyrian kings claim that they captured or killed all the enemy soldiers. For instance, "The inhabitants (subjects) of the city of Hirimme, wicked enemies, who from of old had not submitted to my yoke, I cut down with the sword. Not a soul escaped."[6] If Assyria accomplished a military objective without a total victory, the record will read something like this: "The overthrow of Tirhakah king of Ethiopia he had accomplished, and scattered his forces."[7] The king gets the credit for brilliance. Poor Tirhakah has lost his throne. Tirhakah's soldiers, however, fare much better than the unfortunate members of Hirimme's army—though not through any charity from Ashurbanipal, who wanted to annihilate them too. It is noteworthy, then, that Nahum concludes with a description of the people of Nineveh fleeing or sleeping, but not dead. Unlike Ashurbanipal, God had the power to kill them all. And unlike Ashurbanipal, God chose to spare many of them.

GOD'S MERCY

This brings us back to the question of why God spared them. The answer is plain. God must fulfill his word. He had promised,

In that day there will be a highway from Egypt to Assyria, and Assyria will come into Egypt, and Egypt into Assyria, and the Egyptians will worship with the Assyrians.

> In that day Israel will be the third with Egypt and
> Assyria, a blessing in the midst of the earth, whom
> the LORD of hosts has blessed, saying, "Blessed be
> Egypt my people, and Assyria the work of my hands,
> and Israel my inheritance." (Isa. 19:23–25)

Isaiah had prophesied the redemption of Assyria. The words
of Nahum worked to that end. Nahum does not contradict Isaiah. Nahum does not even contradict Jonah, as so
many are fond of saying. Isaiah, Jonah, and Nahum provide
a consistent message regarding Assyria. God desires the
redemption of Assyria, so that the Assyrian people may
worship him. This redemption requires the destruction
of the evil human and supernatural power structures that
have controlled Assyria throughout most of its history. In
the time of Jonah, the leader of Nineveh humbled himself
before God and found mercy. In the times of Isaiah and
Nahum, the Assyrian leadership did not and was cut off.
The predictions of all three prophets came about. God liberated the Assyrians.

NINEVITE REACTIONS

This brings us to our second question. How did the
average Ninevite respond to the city's fall? This answer is
not so clear, yet we do see three similarities to the events
in Hungary in 1989. In both Nineveh and Hungary, the
totalitarian regimes failed to act. In both Nineveh and Hungary, the gates opened. In both Nineveh and Hungary,
many people left.

We have discussed the incapacitation of the masculine
enemies in Nahum—both the group and the lone male. The
other two issues deserve explanation. The first reference to
gates comes in 2:6, where "the river gates are opened." Now
Nineveh has been besieged. If the gates are opened, it is so
the invading army can get in, right? Maybe the river gates

are opened to unleash a torrent of water to bring down the wall. We have some historical cause to accept this theory. What does Nahum himself think about these gates opening? He tells us in 2:8, "Nineveh is like a pool whose waters run away. 'Halt! Halt!' they cry, but none turns back." The Hebrew word used for "gates" occurs over three hundred times in the Old Testament. Only here do the gates pertain to water. When a gated body of water becomes ungated, which direction does the water flow? In Nineveh, it flowed out. Therefore, the water was inside of Nineveh. The second line of 2:8 confirms this interpretation, as the flowing water imagery gives way to a human exodus. According to verses 6 and 8, the gates of Nineveh kept people in—not out. The army of God opens the gates, the inhabitants flee, the impotent Assyrian leadership commands them to stop, and none obey. When "gates" and "bars" appear again in 3:13, they are "open" and "devoured." To what effect? We learn in the space of the next five verses that the merchants, princes, scribes, and people have all taken the same opportunity that the East Germans did. They left.

The gates did not just hold people in. Nineveh was full of both money (2:9) and corpses (2:12–3:3). Nahum gives us a consistent message. The Assyrian powers used the gates of the city to dam up people and plunder. God's army came to break these powers and tear down these walls. He sent his scatterer to liberate the spiritual concentration camp.

I now want to consider the slave girls in 2:7. I believe that what I have said above comes through well in the English text. This will not. The ESV speaks of "her slave girls lamenting, moaning like doves and beating their breasts." This is a reasonable translation, but each of the seven Hebrew words that Nahum uses here could be interpreted positively or negatively.[8] I think he intended this ambiguity, so that the verse contains two different meanings. Here is an overly wooden translation that illustrates the ambiguity: "and her handmaids leading away as the voice of doves beating upon their hearts."

First, I think Nahum alludes to the story of David, Abigail, and Nabal here. In 1 Samuel 25, David receives an insult from Nabal and sets out to destroy his household. Nabal's wife, Abigail, shows the wisdom and discretion that her husband lacked and intercepts David, offering him gifts and entreating him to refrain from bloodshed. In the midst of Abigail's speech, she calls herself David's handmaid six times—using the same Hebrew word that the ESV translates "slave girls" here. Nahum 2:7 and 3:4–7 both refer to the desecration of the Assyrian queen. In 3:6, we find the word "nabal." Nabal's name means "fool." Nahum 3:6 uses a verb form, which the ESV translates "and treat you with contempt." In both Nahum and 1 Samuel, God destroyed a "nabal" so that a "handmaid" may be set free.

Second, the word translated "dove" in 2:7 is also the name Jonah. In Hebrew, *Jonah* means "dove." Interestingly, both prophets include the other's name in their text. Nahum means "compassion," and the verb form appears in Jonah 3:9, 10; 4:2, where the ESV translates it "relent," "relented," and "relenting."[9] I believe that Nahum used Jonah's name to associate these handmaids with the Ninevites who had repented a hundred years before. Whether the handmaids sing for joy or cry in lament depends on how we interpret the common Hebrew word for "voice," which allows either interpretation.

Third, Nahum chose a curious word to describe the motion of these girls' hands. The word for "beating" appears in only one other place in the Old Testament. When a poet of the magnitude of Nahum picks a word like that, we must consider the possibility that he is alluding to the other text. That text certainly supports my theory:

> Your procession is seen, O God,
> the procession of my God, my King, into the sanctuary—
> the singers in front, the musicians last,
> between them virgins playing [beating] tambourines.
>   (Ps. 68:24–25)

I think Nahum crafted his verse so that it could portray the historical distress of Nineveh's inhabitants as Babylonian soldiers breached its walls, but also so that it could describe the spiritual joy of the Assyrians who have been set free to worship their new God.

TO GLORIFY AND ENJOY

"Man's chief and highest end is to glorify God, and fully to enjoy him for ever." Thus begins the Westminster Larger Catechism, in what may be the most profound theological statement outside of the Bible. All people will glorify God in their lives. Some, however, will more thoroughly fulfill their purpose than others. In Romans 9, we find this:

> What if God, desiring to show his wrath and to make known his power, has endured with much patience vessels of wrath prepared for destruction, in order to make known the riches of his glory for vessels of mercy, which he has prepared beforehand for glory—even us whom he has called, not from the Jews only but also from the Gentiles? (Rom. 9:22–24)

A human being glorifies God by loving and submitting to him—or by suffering eternal judgment as an object of his wrath. God will be glorified by all, but the end for which he created us is that we may fully glorify and enjoy him.

Jesus decreed that "this gospel of the kingdom will be proclaimed throughout the whole world as a testimony to all nations, and then the end will come" (Matt. 24:14). He will not return until all people groups have had the opportunity to hear the gospel. We do not know how to quantify this. Jesus may return before I finish typing this sentence (Mark 13:33). We do know that despite the depravity of humanity, in all its forms, God desires that all people hear the gospel.

Students of Nahum have often interpreted the statements of God's wrath and the descriptions of violent scenes as the single-minded violence of an angry God. A careful reading does not bear this out. Isaiah had prophesied that the gospel would go to Assyria. Nahum was the voice crying out to Assyria, "Prepare the way of the Lord" (Luke 3:4).

FOR FURTHER REFLECTION

1. Has the discussion of this chapter affected how you see the themes of Nahum? If so, in what ways?
2. What characteristics of God does the book of Nahum highlight? Do these make you love God more or less? Do they make you uncomfortable? Why or why not?
3. Read the book of Jonah in light of God's treatment of Nineveh in the book of Nahum. What similarities do you see between the books? What differences?

CHAPTER FIFTEEN

THE PRINCE OF DARKNESS (3:18–19)

The Prince of Darkness grim,
we tremble not for him;
his rage we can endure,
for lo, his doom is sure;
one little word shall fell him.
(Martin Luther)[1]

The two final verses in Nahum piqued my attention ten years ago and started my fascination with the book. The story requires a little background. I began working on a Ph.D. in biblical interpretation in 1999. After I had finished most of my coursework, I took a position as pastor of a church in West Virginia. I still had a few classes to manage, a number of hoops to jump through, comprehensive exams to take, and a dissertation to write. The comprehensive exams had two parts. One was a general exam that all doctoral students took, and the other tested my knowledge of the portion of the Bible I chose to focus on. I wanted to study the prophets, and particularly how the Minor Prophets related to each other, but there was much that I didn't know.

I preached through as many prophetic books as my congregation would tolerate. Many have noted that the best way to learn a subject is to teach it, so I doubled up my sermon preparation and my exam studies. Early on in this process, I did a sermon series on Nahum. Mercifully, if those sermons were recorded, they have now been lost. I muddled through it as best I could.

I remember only one thing from that sermon series. When I worked on Nahum 3:18-19, I became convinced that these verses prophesied Satan's destruction. The sentence "There is no easing your hurt; your wound is grievous" (Nah 3:19) reminded me of God's curse of the serpent in Genesis 3:15. This idea became the seed out of which my studies in Nahum began.

I tell you these memories in order to introduce the question that our last chapter will address: does Nahum 3:18-19 prophesy against a human or a supernatural foe? The answer to this question speaks to the ongoing relevance of Nahum in the biblical canon. You see, most have consigned Nahum to a redundant role in the Bible. Books about Nahum agree on three things. First, Nahum wrote really well. Second, Nahum teaches that God judges evil. Third, the things that Nahum prophesied have all happened. What relevance do these three points have to the people sitting in the pew on Sunday morning? Well, it may cause them to be thankful for the literary beauty of the Scriptures. It warns them of the dangers of sin. It comforts them that God will see that justice is done. It also provides a remarkable testimony of the inerrancy of Scripture, since numerous details of Nahum's prophecy were fulfilled exactly. These are good points, but points that could be made from many books of the Bible.

Let me put it to you another way. What have the Assyrians done to you lately? The historical fulfillment of Nahum's words was so complete that for a while scholars doubted the veracity of the biblical account. Little was known about Assyria before two hundred years ago. They were a cruel empire, but God judged them. How does this book relate to today? It relates to us because we have an ancient foe.

"Then the dragon became furious with the woman and went off to make war on the rest of her offspring, on those who keep the commandments of God and hold to the testimony of Jesus" (Rev. 12:17).

KING ASSHUR

It has taken until the final two verses to discover the identity of the mysterious male in the book of Nahum. In two verses of taunts, Nahum speaks to the "king of Assyria." He is the one whose yoke is broken (1:13). He is the one whose line dies out (1:14). He is the one futilely directing Nineveh's defense (2:5). He is the one who has to watch Nineveh's destruction (2:7).

The identification of this figure with Ashurbanipal, or with another human king, has problems, however. We have seen that Nahum knew Assyria and its ideology. Many places in the prophecy have reversed Assyrian boasts. Two aspects of verse 18 disqualify a human king as the ultimate target of the taunts.

First, the verse begins by referring to "your shepherds." Dating back to early history, the kings in Mesopotamia took the title "shepherd." For instance, in the famous Code of Hammurabi, King Hammurabi identifies himself as "Hammurabi, the shepherd, called by Enlil."[2] Closer to Nahum's time, the Assyrian kings Tiglath-pileser III, Sargon II, Sennacherib, Esarhaddon, and Ashurbanipal all used this title. In Assyrian ideology, the titles *king* and *shepherd* were interchangeable.

The title *shepherd* paradoxically exalted the king above all his subjects while also humbling him below all his gods. In Mesopotamian religion, a great chasm existed between humanity and divinity. All of the king's subjects bowed to his whims. Yet Mesopotamian rulers seemed genuinely to cower before the will of their gods—the Assyrians particularly so. We may contrast this with the Egyptian tradition, in which Pharaoh was viewed as divine. The Assyrians served their king, who was but a human servant of the great god Asshur.

The Assyrian people belonged to Asshur. The Assyrian Empire existed for his glory. Assyrian armies marched out to expand Asshur's influence. He appointed the man who would shepherd the people. Assyrian kings claimed, not to be god, but to have been chosen by Asshur for a sacred task: the care of his people.

Nahum disputed this claim. Assyrian kings did not shepherd; they devoured (2:11–13). The Assyrian notion of the shepherd-king deeply perverted the ideal given in Psalm 23. All those in authority who do not truly submit to Christ use that authority for their own purposes. Satan will counterfeit Christ in every way. He will pretend to be a shepherd. We must guard ourselves against those who only pretend to shepherd us for our benefit. We must give the care of our soul only to the true "Shepherd and Overseer of [our] souls" (1 Peter 2:25). We must also die to self so that we may truly be a shepherd for Christ.

> The greatest among you shall be your servant. Whoever exalts himself will be humbled, and whoever humbles himself will be exalted. (Matt. 23:11–12)

Nahum's phrase "your shepherds" leaves us in a dilemma. Either he chose the word carelessly or we need to accept that the taunts of 3:18–19 target King Asshur, the Assyrian high war-god. As you have guessed, I prefer the latter explanation.

While "your shepherds" identifies the mysterious adversary as Asshur, Nahum 3:18 provides additional evidence for this interpretation. The second sentence of the verse reads, "Your people are scattered on the mountains with none to gather them." Again, Nahum uses a conspicuous reference to Assyrian kings as shepherds, but with a more specific job description. The Assyrian shepherd-king lived to serve Asshur. Asshur charged each king with gathering his people.

This task of "gathering" included two different yet related duties. First, the Assyrian king had to gather the armies to march out to war. For instance,

> In my fourth expedition, I gathered my army.[3]

> My men of war I gathered, and I took the march.[4]

> In the service of Assur and Nergal the Gods my protectors a second time I gathered my army.[5]

> In my ninth expedition I gathered my army, against Vaiteh king of Arabia.[6]

Preparing such military expeditions required effort and planning. Assyria used soldiers from throughout its realm. These armies needed immense supply trains. This task fell to the shepherd-king, who gathered Asshur's forces for war.

Second, when the armies went out, they gathered foreign nations into the empire. "I, Esarhaddon, king of Assyria, the humble king, the exalted prince, favorite of the great gods, gathered together the peoples of the lands which my hands had conquered."[7] Ultimately, this was done for the glory of Asshur. The historian Michael Burger explains that in Mesopotamia "all war . . . was holy war. Moreover, other peoples, like the Assyrians, believed that their patron god was not just one among many, but the ruler over all the other gods. The Assyrians, however, seemed readier to take their ideas to the logical conclusion, that what was so in heaven must be made so on earth."[8] All peoples belonged in Asshur's sheepfold. The king gathered the army in order to gather the nations.

Our earlier discussions of Nahum 1:9–12, 14; 2:7 support this interpretation as well. In these verses, Nahum declares the masculine singular enemy incapacitated, yet alert. He has no power to act. In contrast, God has incapacitated the masculine plural enemies by taking away their alertness. Nahum describes them as sleeping (3:18) drunkards (1:10).

We may therefore surmise that Nahum primarily speaks the judgment of 3:18-19 to a supernatural being. We may also surmise that these verses prophesy the end of Assyria's deified patriarch. The words that the ESV translates as "king of Assyria" could also be rendered "King Asshur." Nahum's allusions to Genesis 10-11 demonstrate his familiarity with Assyria's origins. Assyria and the god Asshur took their names from Asshur, son of Shem. The Assyrians merely came to treat their common human ancestor as the great god of the universe.

The Bible and history agree. Something happened in 639 B.C. that made Assyria unresponsive to Asshur's incessant lust for conquest. The Assyrian shepherd-kings slept. The Assyrian aristocracy slumbered. Asshur's scattered people had no shepherd to gather them. The armies had no purpose. The vassals wandered from the fold. We can only guess how this happened. Somehow this warrior people lost its stomach for war. Perhaps a life of luxury overcame them. One way or another, they no longer did Asshur's will.

THE WOUND

By mere verbal fiat—set in motion by a humble Judean—the greatest empire in the world rotted and crumbled. In Nahum's final verse, we find the judgment already begun but not yet completed. This evil being has suffered a mortal blow. Nothing can reverse this. As we finish the book, he remains in this incapacitated state. He will not heal. His best days are gone. But the battle is not yet finished.

When we read Nahum 3:19 from the perspective of the New Testament, we find a prophecy of Satan's demise. In Genesis 3, God had promised that one of Eve's line would crush Satan's head. We now know that that one was Christ.

At the cross, Jesus "disarmed the rulers and authorities and put them to open shame" (Col. 2:15). Though he was defeated at the cross, Satan's demise remains incomplete. He still makes war against the children of God. He still seeks to devour them. Fortunately, God's elect now have weapons to overcome him "by the blood of the Lamb and by the word of their testimony" (Rev. 12:11).

The day of final victory lies in the future. In that day, Satan and his servants will be "thrown into the lake of fire and sulfur where the beast and the false prophet were, and they will be tormented day and night forever and ever" (Rev. 20:10). Nahum prophesied this moment.

Yes, we live in a time when Assyrian chariots are a distant memory. Empires have come and gone. The methods of cruelty have evolved. The tyrants have technology. Nahum testifies that God sees and judges. God will hold humans responsible for their evil. The Bible speaks of a greater enemy who has done more evil. For this reason, persecuted Christians can pray for and love their tormentors. They know that God will avenge their blood, and they know that their real enemy is not of this world. The book of Nahum remains as applicable today as it was to its first recipients. In fact, today we may read it with greater understanding and benefit than they did.

From the perspective of the New Testament, we see that the ultimate adversary in this book is "that ancient serpent, who is called the devil and Satan" (Rev. 12:9). His "wound is grievous" (Nah. 3:19) due to Jesus' victory at the cross. Though he still prowls, Jesus has given us weapons not only to withstand his attacks but to invade his territory and plunder his possessions.

ALL WHO HEAR

I have titled this book *Severe Compassion: The Gospel According to Nahum*. The term "severe compassion" comes from the meaning behind the Hebrew words for "Nahum of Elkosh" (1:1). The book of Nahum contains the message of God's great compassion for us. That compassion will take on a severe nature when God's people stray from him into destructive paths. I understand this from my own experience. God has chastened me many times. I see in hindsight the danger of those situations. I recoil in realizing how blind I was to the danger. I also understand severe compassion because I am a father. I love my children. If the day should come that any of them would decide to walk away from God, I would pray day and night that God would use any means necessary to bring them back. If he did so, I would be grateful—no matter what the cost.

Psalm 32:8–9 speaks about God's methods of discipline. It reads,

> I will instruct you and teach you in the way you
>   should go;
> I will counsel you with my eye upon you.
> Be not like a horse or a mule, without understanding,
>   which must be curbed with bit and bridle,
>   or it will not stay near you.

I know almost nothing about horses, but I have a daughter who loves them. The little that I do know has come from her influence. There have been many days when the television implanted equestrian dressage into my subconscious. I have learned that an expert rider on a well-trained horse can control the horse with nearly imperceptible signals. Psalm 32 speaks thus of us. God desires that we hear and obey the word of Psalm 32:8. He counsels and we comply. If this method proves ineffective, he proceeds to Psalm 32:9: bit, bridle, and then even more severe discipline, if necessary.

The book of Nahum begins at the end of Judah's affliction. They had rebelled and gone after other gods. God gave them over to the consequences of their behavior. But the gospel according to Nahum only begins there. God soon pronounces Judah free. He has chastened his people and now delivers them from physical and spiritual bondage.

The book of Nahum speaks to us of even more profound realities. We have given ourselves more completely to the great whore (Rev. 17–18) and Satan than Judah ever gave itself to Assyria. We have suffered under a greater tyrant. God in his mercy allows us to suffer the consequences of our actions. He allows us to feel the misery that comes with this slavery. He also sent his Son to break the power of sin, death, hell, and Satan in order to set us free. Jesus took the sin of his sheep, drank the cup of God's wrath, suffered the torments of hell, and rose victorious from the grave. He has mortally wounded our enemy. Nahum preaches this gospel.

Each book of the Bible makes a unique contribution. None is redundant. Nahum speaks of God's great love for his adulterous people. It speaks of his willingness to enter history in order to overthrow the seductive powers that lured his bride away. It speaks of his relentless pursuit of any who would compete for her affections. It comforts Christ's bride that the powers of hell are broken.

This gospel message culminates in the prophecy's final four lines. The better we understand the evil of sin and the more we have learned to hate our captor, the more we will rejoice at the news that "lo, his doom is sure." Nahum 3:19 preaches a fuller gospel than this, though. It mirrors the heart of God found in the last lines of Jonah. Both of these Minor Prophets end with rhetorical questions that show God's heart for the nations. Nahum's message is universal: "All who hear the news about you clap their hands over you. For upon whom has not come your unceasing evil?" (3:19).

Jesus said, "The harvest is plentiful" (Matt. 9:37). Nahum 3:19 concurs. The whole world groans under Satan's tyranny. People from "every nation and tribe and language and people" (Rev. 14:6) long to be delivered. Jesus has equipped his church with everything it needs to open the gates and bars of Satan's kingdom and to let them go free. When they are set free, they will rejoice. Unfortunately, Jesus also said that "the laborers are few" (Matt. 9:37). We have lots of professional clergy. We have many missionaries. We have many church officers and church edifices. Do we have many laborers who live a crucified life in order to set people free, becoming experts in the use of spiritual weapons?

Nahum teaches us about the horror of sin and the love of Christ. It tells us about our helplessness and Christ's power. It reveals Satan's frailty in the face of God's true church. It also speaks of God's love for a broken world. "May the Lamb that was slain receive the reward of his suffering."

FOR FURTHER REFLECTION

1. Nahum prophesied that Satan's power would be broken. How do we see this fulfilled in the New Testament?
2. How sensitive are you to God's instruction? How do you know God's will for you? How does he "counsel you" (Ps. 32:8)?
3. Has reading this book changed your perception of Satan? How?
4. Many nations live in darkness, without ready access to the Bible or the gospel. Research one and pray for this nation.
5. Are you willing to surrender your life in every way, that Christ may receive the glory due his name? Will you now ask God to change you in whatever way he needs to? Will you ask him to give you a burning passion to glorify him and to fully enjoy him forever?

NOTES

CHAPTER ONE: JEALOUS LOVE

1 Robert Lowth, *Lectures on the Sacred Poetry of the Hebrews*, trans. G. Gregory (Boston: Crocker & Brewer, 1829), 180.

2 Lynell Zogbo and Ernst R. Wendland, *Hebrew Poetry in the Bible: A Guide for Understanding and Translating*, Helps for Translators (New York: United Bible Societies, 2000), 2.

3 Richard D. Weis, "The Genre *Maśśā'* in the Hebrew Bible" (PhD diss., Claremont Graduate School, 1986), 273.

CHAPTER TWO: RESTORATION

1 DC Talk and The Voice of the Martyrs, *Jesus Freaks: Stories of Those Who Stood for Jesus; The Ultimate Jesus Freaks* (Tulsa, OK: Albury, 1999), 260.

2 The Neo-Assyrian "period is technically a linguistic designation, denoting the third and last period of the Assyrian dialect of Akkadian (Old Assyrian period c.2000–c.1800 B.C.E.; Middle Assyrian period c.1400–c.1050 B.C.E.), although this period is coincident with the empire in which the texts are generated. While dates for the beginning of the empire can be disputed, it is generally accepted that the empire existed from the late tenth century until the late seventh century (c.954–c.605 B.C.E.), more than three hundred years. It was therefore also the most durable empire seen until then in western Asia" (Peter R. Bedford, "The Neo-Assyrian Empire," in *The Dynamics of Ancient Empires: State Power from Assyria to Byzantium*, ed. Ian Morris and Walter Scheidel [Oxford: Oxford University Press, 2009], 30).

3 This insight comes from chapter 6 of Bill Cooper's Kindle book, *The Authenticity of the Book of Jonah*, 2012.

4 "Sennacherib (704–681)," in *Ancient Near Eastern Texts Relating to the Old Testament*, ed. James B. Pritchard, 3rd ed. (Princeton: Princeton University Press, 1969), 288. (Parentheses, brackets, and italics, placed in Assyrian texts here and hereafter, are original.)

CHAPTER THREE: GOD COMES TO EARTH

1 See the Nicene Creed.

2 Jonathan Edwards, *The Religious Affections* (1746; repr., Mineola, NY: Dover, 2013), 60.

3 Elisabeth Elliot, *Shadow of the Almighty: The Life and Testament of Jim Elliot* (1958; repr., Peabody, MA: Hendrickson, 2008), 330.

4 The most interesting and outlandish of these comes from the Greek historian Diodorus (90–30 B.C.). His account focuses on a debauched king, Sardanapallus (2.23–27). It is difficult to ascertain the validity of what seems to be a legendary account. In this story, an ancient prophecy stated that Nineveh would never fall until the river turned against the city. When the swollen river causes the wall to collapse, Sardanapallus despairs and immolates himself and his concubines. See Diodorus Siculus, *Library of History: Books 1–2.34*, trans. C. H. Oldfather (Cambridge: Harvard University Press, 1933), 439–43, available online at http://penelope.uchicago.edu/Thayer/E/Roman /Texts/Diodorus_Siculus/2A*.html.

5 "The Epic of Gilgamesh," in *Myths from Mesopotamia*, trans. Stephanie Dalley (Oxford: Oxford University Press, 1991), 89.

CHAPTER FOUR: NAHUM AND PSALM 9

1 Chris Baldick, *The Oxford Dictionary of Literary Terms* (Oxford: Oxford University Press, 2008), 26.

2 Oswald T. Allis, "Nahum, Nineveh, Elkosh," *Evangelical Quarterly* 27, no. 2 (April 1955): 73.

3 "The didactic poet looks upon the series of the elements of language as the flight of steps, up which he leads his pupil to the sanctuary of wisdom, or as the many celled casket in which he puts the pearls of the teaching of his wisdom; the lyric poet looks upon them as the keyboard, on which he strikes every key, in order to give the fullest expression to his emotions; even the prophet does not disdain, as is evident from Nah. i. 3–7, to allow the sequence of the letters

of the alphabet to have an influence upon the arrangement of his thoughts" (Franz Delitzsch, *A Commentary on the Book of Psalms*, vol. 1 [1883; repr., London: Forgotten Books, 2013], 205).

4   Michael H. Floyd, "The Chimerical Acrostic of Nahum 1:2–10," *Journal of Biblical Literature* 113, no. 3 (1994): 430 (italics in original).

5   Julia M. O'Brien, *Nahum*, 2nd ed., Readings (London: Sheffield Academic, 2009), 105.

6   John Merlin Powis Smith, William Hayes Ward, and Julius A. Bewer, *A Critical and Exegetical Commentary on Micah, Zephaniah, Nahum, Habakkuk, Obadiah and Joel*, International Critical Commentary (New York: Charles Scribner's Sons, 1911), 273–74.

7   "The psalm is an incomplete acrostic psalm (*aleph–kaph*) and seems to have formally belonged together with Psalm 10 (*lamed–taw*). There are several arguments given in support of treating these two psalms as a unit: (1) the absence of a superscription in Psalm 10, (2) the continuity of the acrostic device, (3) similar vocabulary, and (4) the LXX's and Vulgate's treatment of Psalms 9 and 10 as one psalm.

"Over against this, however, we observe that the acrostic pattern is incomplete and may have been imposed on one psalm. Psalm 9 seems to be a complete unit of itself" (William A. VanGemeren, *Psalms*, Expositor's Bible Commentary 5, ed. Tremper Longman III and David E. Garland, rev. ed. [Grand Rapids: Zondervan, 2008], 143).

8   Robert Alter, *The Book of Psalms: A Translation with Commentary* (New York: W. W. Norton, 2007), 25.

CHAPTER FIVE: DISARMED

1   Daniel David Luckenbill, *Ancient Records of Assyria and Babylonia*, vol. 2, *Historical Records of Assyria from Sargon to the End* (Chicago: University of Chicago Press, 1927), 13.

2   "Sennacherib (704–681)," in *Ancient Near Eastern Texts Relating to the Old Testament*, ed. James B. Pritchard, 3rd ed. (Princeton: Princeton University Press, 1969), 288.

3   Luckenbill, *Ancient Records*, 2:310.

4   "Rabshakeh" was a title given to one of the highest ranking officials in the Assyrian government. We do not know the precise nature of the job. These officials find their way into Assyrian accounts, such

as, "I ordered to add to my former (battle-)forces (in Egypt) the *rabšaq*-officer, all the governors (and) kings of (the region) beyond the river" ("Ashurbanipal [668–633]," in Pritchard, *Ancient Near Eastern Texts*, 296).

5 "The death of Ashurbanipal was immediately followed by widespread outbreaks of unrest. Josiah's activities were probably an aspect of this, for, according to 2 Chronicles 34:6, it was immediately afterwards, in his twelfth year (628 B.C.), that he assumed control of the Assyrian province comprising Samaria, Gilead, and Galilee. Such virtual rebellion would, under a strong Assyrian government, have evoked rigorous action. That this did not ensue was because Assyria faced more serious trouble in Babylonia, where by 626 B.C. a certain Nabopolassar, of Chaldean descent, was able to assume kingship" (H. W. F. Saggs, "The Assyrians," in *Peoples of Old Testament Times*, ed. D. J. Wiseman [Oxford: Clarendon, 1973], 166).

"Assyrian royal inscriptions and archival material are very sparse for this period. This must partly be due to succession problems in Assyria: the evidence shows that the hold on the throne of Ashurbanipal's heir Ashur-etel-ilani, was contested; he was eventually succeeded by his brother, Sin-shar-ishkun. At one point, even one of his officials (or eunuchs), Sin-shum-lishir, briefly claimed the throne. . . . All that is certain is that Ashur-etel-ilani succeeded Ashurbanipal on the throne; that his brother, Sin-shar-ishkun, ruled until 612; that the official, Sin-shum-lishir, claimed the kingship at some point before Sin-shar-ishkun's accession; finally that the Babylonian general, Nabopolassar, claimed the Babylonian throne in 626 and was in undisputed control there by 616" (Amélie Kuhrt, *The Ancient Near East c. 3000–330 BC*, Routledge History of the Ancient World [New York: Routledge, 1995], 2:541).

6 George Smith, *History of Assurbanipal, Translated from the Cuneiform Inscriptions* (London: Williams & Norgate, 1871), 69.

7 Ibid., 23.

8 Ashurbanipal's "enthusiasm for reading and writing, which he seems to have shared with his wife, Libbāli-šarrat, can be traced back to his youth. From an autobiographical sketch about his intellectual socialization, we know that Ashurbanipal had received the education of a future scholar" (Eckart Frahm, "Royal Hermeneutics:

Observations on the Commentaries from Ashurbanipal's Libraries at Nineveh," *Iraq* 66 [2004]: 45).

9 "The sources for Assyrian history cease to speak to us for the last dozen years of Assurbanipal's rule. It seems that the empire had already begun to disintegrate during his lifetime, and it disappeared with appalling speed under the short-lived rule of his successor and son" (A. Leo Oppenheim, *Ancient Mesopotamia: Portrait of a Dead Civilization*, rev. ed. by Erica Reiner [Chicago: University of Chicago Press, 1977], 169–70).

CHAPTER SIX: GOOD NEWS

1 "Of all the oppressive imperial powers that have stained the pages of human history from the past to the present, Assyria claims a place of pre-eminence among evil nations. It was a nation with a long history, but during the first millennium B.C. it embarked upon a path of imperial expansion which knew no limitations of human decency and kindness. And among the many nations that experienced Assyria's cruelty, its invasion of territory and its ruthless military methods, the small state of Judah was but one" (Peter C. Craigie, *Twelve Prophets, vol. 2: Micah, Nahum, Habakkuk, Zephaniah, Haggai, Zechariah, and Malachi*, Daily Study Bible Series [Louisville: Westminster John Knox Press, 1985], 58).

2 Daniel David Luckenbill, *Ancient Records of Assyria and Babylonia*, vol. 2, *Historical Records of Assyria from Sargon to the End* (Chicago: University of Chicago Press, 1927), 82.

3 Gordon H. Johnston, "Nahum's Rhetorical Allusions to Neo-Assyrian Conquest Metaphors," *Bibliotheca Sacra* 159 (2002): 27. For instance, "I led my armies from one end of the earth to the other and brought in submission at my feet all princes, dwelling in palaces, of the four quarters (of the world),—and they assumed (*lit.*, drew) my yoke" (Luckenbill, *Ancient Records*, 2:195).

4 I recommend the Open Richly Annotated Cuneiform Corpus (http://oracc.museum.upenn.edu/). This project of the University of Pennsylvania has extensive translations of Assyrian texts. The Vassal Treaty of Esarhaddon is found at http://oracc.museum.upenn.edu/saao/saa02/P336598. The curses start about two-thirds of the way through the document.

5   C. S. Lewis provided an excellent illustration of this in *The Lion, the Witch, and the Wardrobe*. In that book, Edmund betrays his siblings, Aslan, and Narnia for some Turkish Delight. Lucy intercedes with Aslan to save him: "'Please—Aslan . . . can anything be done to save Edmund?'
    "'All shall be done,' said Aslan. 'But it may be harder than you think'" (C. S. Lewis, *The Lion, the Witch, and the Wardrobe* [1950; repr., New York: HarperTrophy, 1994], 141).

6   Archibald H. Sayce, *Assyria: Its Princes, Priests, and People* (New York: Fleming H. Revell, 1893), 83–84.

7   Lewis Spence, *Myths & Legends of Babylonia & Assyria* (London: George G. Harrap, 1916), 211.

8   Twila Paris, "How Beautiful," *Cry for the Desert*, Star Song, 1990, compact disc. Used by permission.

CHAPTER SEVEN: THE WEAPONS OF OUR WARFARE

1   Elizabeth Achtemeier, *Nahum–Malachi*, Interpretation: A Bible Commentary for Teaching and Preaching (Louisville: Westminster John Knox Press, 1986), 18.

2   Martin Luther, "A Mighty Fortress Is Our God," 1529; trans. Frederick H. Hedge, 1853.

3   Jonathan Edwards, "Hypocrites Deficient in the Duty of Prayer," (sermon, June 1740), available online at http://www.ccel.org/ccel /edwards/sermons.hypocrites.html.

4   Ibid.

5   Rosalind Goforth, *How I Know God Answers Prayer: The Personal Testimony of One Life-Time* (Philadelphia: Sunday School Times, 1921), 15–16.

6   J. Hudson Taylor, "The Source of Power for Christian Missions," *The Missionary Review of the World*, 13.1 (1900): 516.

7   Joel R. Beeke and Sinclair B. Ferguson, eds., *Reformed Confessions Harmonized* (Grand Rapids: Baker, 1999), 26–27.

CHAPTER EIGHT: REVERSAL

1   C. S. Lewis, *The Lion, the Witch, and the Wardrobe* (1950; repr., New York: HarperTrophy, 1994), 153.

2 Godfrey R. Driver, "Farewell to Queen Huzzab!" *Journal of Theological Studies* 15, no. 2 (1964): 296–98.

3 Joseph Reider, "A New Ishtar Epithet in the Bible," *Journal of Near Eastern Studies* 8, no. 2 (April 1949): 104.

4 Driver's solution to the Huzzab puzzle involved combining "an adequate knowledge of Greek and Arabic vocabularies with sufficient imagination to explain a rare or unique Hebrew term" (Driver, "Farewell to Queen Huzzab!" 297). Even though this explanation seems mild compared with other outlandish suggestions, it still requires unnecessary mental gymnastics.

5 The idea that a humiliated king is forced to watch this scene is not original to me. It has been proposed before from a different perspective. For instance, see Klaas Spronk, *Nahum*, Historical Commentary on the Old Testament (Kampen, The Netherlands: Kok Pharos, 1997), 96.

6 John Piper, "George Mueller's Strategy for Showing God: Simplicity of Faith, Sacred Scripture, and Satisfaction in God," *Desiring God*, February 3, 2004, http://www.desiringgod.org/biographies/george-muellers-strategy-for-showing-god. See esp. note 28.

7 Arthur T. Pierson, *George Müller of Bristol* (London: James Nisbet & Co., 1899), 138 (italics in original).

8 George Müller, *A Narrative of Some of the Lord's Dealings with George Müller: First Part*, 3rd. ed. (Bristol: J. Nisbet & Co., 1845), 146.

CHAPTER NINE: THE GOOD SHEPHERD

1 See the wall reliefs from Nineveh in the British Museum.

2 John Bunyan, *Pilgrim's Progress* (1678; repr., Grand Rapids: Baker, 1984), 96.

3 Ibid, 105.

CHAPTER TEN: THE SHADOW OF DEATH

1 H. W. F. Saggs, *The Might That Was Assyria* (London: Sidgwick & Jackson, 1984), 116.

2 "Ashurbanipal (668–633)," in *Ancient Near Eastern Texts Relating to the Old Testament*, ed. James B. Pritchard, 3rd ed. (Princeton: Princeton University Press, 1969), 300.

3   Daniel David Luckenbill, *Ancient Records of Assyria and Babylonia*, vol. 2, *Historical Records of Assyria from Sargon to the End* (Chicago: University of Chicago Press, 1927), 127.

4   "That is, the dead bodies of verse 3 are the result of Assyria's evil trickery of her foreign neighbors. . . . [T]here is a repetition in the Hebrew of '*kabod*,' in 2:9, where it refers to Nineveh's 'heaps' of treasure, and in 3:3, where it depicts the 'heaps' of corpses that she has caused" (Elizabeth Achtemeier, *Nahum–Malachi*, Interpretation: A Bible Commentary for Teaching and Preaching [Louisville: Westminster John Knox Press, 1986], 23). In royal inscriptions, Assyrian kings boasted of the piles of bodies that resulted from their military feats. One of Ashurbanipal's inscriptions reads, "I removed the corpses of those whom the pestilence had felled, whose leftovers (after) the dogs and pigs had fed on them were obstructing the streets, filling the places (of Babylon), (and) of those who had lost their lives through the terrible famine" ("The Death of Sennacherib," in Pritchard, *Ancient Near Eastern Texts*, 288).

5   Lewis E. Jones, "There Is Power in the Blood," 1899.

6   Ibid.

7   James Proctor, "It Is Finished!" n.d.

8   Seth L. Sanders, "The First Tour of Hell: From Neo-Assyrian Propaganda to Early Jewish Revelation," *Journal of Ancient Near Eastern Religions* 9, no. 2 (2009): 151.

9   There seems to be a range of opinion. Seth Sanders bases his conclusions on Ashurbanipal being the prince. Mehmet-Ali Ataç takes a more cautious approach: "It describes the night vision of one Kumma, who may be Ashurbanipal, though this is not certain" ("The 'Underworld Vision' of the Ninevite Intellectual Milieu," *Iraq* 66 [2004]: 69). Alasdair Livingstone, who translated the text, remarks, "The language is Standard Babylonian, and the form and style are similar to those of epic. However, the veiled references to Sennacherib and to court politics bring the work into the category of propaganda. It is possible, though not certain, that the crown prince, referred to by the name Kummâ, is Assurbanipal" (*Court Poetry and Literary Miscellanea*, State Archives of Assyria 3 [Helsinki: Helsinki University Press, 1989], xxviii).

10   "The Descent of Ishtar to the Underworld," trans. Stephanie Dalley, in *The Context of Scripture*, ed. William W. Hallo and K. Lawson Younger, vol. 1, *Canonical Compositions from the Biblical World* (Leiden, Netherlands: Brill, 2003), 381.

11   Jonathan Edwards, "Sinners in the Hands of an Angry God" (sermon, Enfield, CT, July 8, 1741), available online at http://digitalcommons .unl.edu/cgi/viewcontent.cgi?article = 1053&context = etas.

12   George Whitefield, "The Method of Grace," in *Selected Sermons of George Whitefield* (Grand Rapids: Christian Classics Ethereal Library, n.d.), 580, available online at http://www.ccel.org/w/whitefield /sermons/cache/sermons.pdf.

CHAPTER ELEVEN: HUMAN TRAFFICKING

1   David Batstone, *Not for Sale: The Return of the Global Slave Trade—and How We Can Fight It* (New York: HarperCollins, 2007), 1.

2   Julie Galambush, "Nahum," in *The Women's Bible Commentary*, 3rd ed., ed. Carol A. Newsom, Sharon H. Ringe, and Jacqueline E. Lapsely (Louisville: Westminster John Knox Press, 2012), 330.

3   For a more detailed explanation of this hypothesis, please see my article, "Human Trafficking in Nahum," in *Horizons in Biblical Theology* 37, no. 2 (2015), 142–57.

4   United Nations Office on Drugs and Crime, *United Nations Convention against Transnational Organized Crime and the Protocols Thereto* (New York: United Nations, 2004), 42, available online at https://www.unodc.org/documents/middleeastandnorthafrica /organised-crime/UNITED_NATIONS_CONVENTION_AGAINST _TRANSNATIONAL_ORGANIZED_CRIME_AND_THE _PROTOCOLS_THERETO.pdf.

5   Rashida Valika, "Women Trafficking in Pakistan: A Tale of Misery and Exploitation," *Pakistan Journal of Women's Studies* 14, no. 1 (2007): 20.

6   "Traffickers or intermediaries, acting as if they want to assist girls and women, but in reality wanting to deceive them and abuse their vulnerable positions, tell the prospective victims success stories of women who go abroad and earn lots of money" (Oguzhan Omer Demir, "Methods of Sex Trafficking: Findings of a Case Study in Turkey," *Global Crime* 11, no. 3 [2010]: 316).

7   Padam Simkhada, "Life Histories and Survival Strategies amongst Sexually Trafficked Girls in Nepal," *Children & Society* 22, no. 3 (May 2008): 244.

8   See "Tiglath-pileser III: 47," *Royal Inscriptions of the Neo-Assyrian Period 1: Tiglath-pileser III and Shalmaneser V*, accessed March 9, 2016, http://oracc.museum.upenn.edu/rinap/rinap1/corpus/.

9   "Estimates of the overall number of people deported in the [Neo-Assyrian] period range from 1.5 to 4.5 million. But even the lower of these figures is commonly considered to be impossibly high, not least because of the logistical problem facing the Assyrian administration in moving, in the largest contingent, some 208,000 persons" (Peter R. Bedford, "The Neo-Assyrian Empire," in *The Dynamics of Ancient Empires: State Power from Assyria to Byzantium*, ed. Ian Morris and Walter Scheidel [Oxford: Oxford University Press, 2009], 33). Whatever the actual total, the Neo-Assyrian Empire practiced kidnapping on a greater scale than the ancient Near East had ever witnessed.

10   "Black's (1990) law dictionary defines a pimp as someone who obtains customers for a prostitute. The reality of most pimps, however, is that they use manipulation, threats, and violence to keep prostitutes from leaving the trade and live entirely off the women they recruit. Research has consistently revealed that pimps are often perpetrators of violence against prostituted women" (M. Alexis Kennedy et al., "Routes of Recruitment: Pimps' Techniques and Other Circumstances That Lead to Street Prostitution," *Journal of Aggression, Maltreatment & Trauma* 15, no. 2 [2007]: 5).

11   "No matter how these women and girls get into the field of prostitution, it is difficult to get out of it once they are in. Pimps and brothel owners use violence, threats, and addiction to drugs and alcohol to control them, sometimes keeping them in slave-like conditions. Often women can leave prostitution only after they are used-up, become ill, and can no longer make money for the pimps" (Valika, "Pakistan," 22).

12   See "Sennacherib: 017," *Royal Inscriptions of the Neo-Assyrian Period 3: Sennacherib*, accessed March 9, 2016, http://oracc.museum.upenn.edu/rinap/rinap3/corpus/.

13   Ibid.

14 Keith Green, "There Is a Redeemer," by Melody Green, on *Songs for the Shepherd*, Sparrow Records, 1982, CD.

CHAPTER TWELVE: THE GREAT PROSTITUTE

1 Charles Spurgeon said that the majority of Ezekiel 16 "is rather for private reading than for the public assembly" (Charles Spurgeon, "Two Immutable Things" [semon, Metropolitan Tabernacle, London, October 30, 1887], available online at http://www.spurgeongems.org/vols40-42/chs2438.pdf).

2 For instance, Julie Galambush, "Nahum," in *The Women's Bible Commentary*, 3rd ed., ed. Carol A. Newsom, Sharon H. Ringe, and Jacqueline E. Lapsely (Louisville: Westminster John Knox Press, 2012), 332; F. Rachel Magdalene, "Ancient Near Eastern Treaty-Curses and the Ultimate Texts of Terror: A Study of the Language of Divine Sexual Abuse in the Prophetic Corpus," in *The Latter Prophets*, ed. Athalya Brenner, A Feminist Companion to the Bible, 1st ser. (Sheffield, UK: Sheffield Academic, 1995), 333; Gerlinde Baumann, "Prophetic Objections to Yʜwʜ as the Violent Husband of Israel: Reinterpretations of the Prophetic Marriage Metaphor in Second Isaiah (Isaiah 40–55)," in *Prophets and Daniel*, ed. Athalya Brenner, A Feminist Companion to the Bible, 2nd ser. (London: Sheffield Academic Press, 2001), 100.

3 Judith E. Sanderson, "Nahum," in *The Women's Bible Commentary*, ed. Carol A. Newsom and Sharon H. Ringe (Louisville: Westminster/John Knox, 1992), 221.

4 Susan Brooks Thistlethwaite, "'You May Enjoy the Spoil of Your Enemies': Rape as a Biblical Metaphor for War," *Semeia* 61 (1993): 59–75.

5 Mayer I. Gruber, "Nineveh the Adultress," in Brenner, *Prophets and Daniel*, 222.

6 "The Epic of Gilgamesh," in *Myths from Mesopotamia*, trans. Stephanie Dalley (Oxford: Oxford University Press, 1991), 77.

7 Ibid, 78.

8 Ibid, 80.

9 For instance, one of Esarhaddon's inscriptions reads, "I wrote to all of the kings who are in the midst of the sea, from Iadnana (Cyprus) (and) Ionia to Tarsus, (and) they bowed down at my feet. I received

[their] heavy tribute. I achieved victory over the rulers of the four quarters and I sprinkled the venom of death over all of (my) enemies. I carried off gold, silver, goods, possessions, people—young (and) old—horses, oxen, (and) sheep and goats, their heavy booty that was beyond counting, to Assyria" (see "Esarhaddon 060," *Royal Inscriptions of the Neo-Assyrian Period 4: Esarhaddon*, accessed March 9, 2016, http://oracc.museum.upenn.edu/rinap/rinap4/corpus/).

10 Laurel Lanner, *"Who Will Lament Her?": The Feminine and the Fantastic in the Book of Nahum* (New York: T & T Clark, 2006), 147.

11 Simo Parpola and Kazuko Watanabe, *Neo-Assyrian Treaties and Loyalty Oaths*, State Archives of Assyria 2 (Helsinki: Helsinki University Press, 1988), xiii.

12 Zainab Bahrani, *Women of Babylon: Gender and Representation in Mesopotamia* (London: Routledge, 2001), 43.

13 Julian Reade, "The Ishtar Temple at Nineveh," *Iraq* 67 (2005): 347.

14 Julia Assante, "Sex, Magic and the Liminal Body in the Erotic Art and Texts of the Old Babylonian Period," in *Sex and Gender in the Ancient Near East: Proceedings of the 47th Rencontre Assyriologique Internationale, Helsinki, July 2–6, 2001*, vol. 1, ed. Simo Parpola and Robert M. Whiting (Helsinki: Neo-Assyrian Text Corpus Project, 2002), 48.

15 Nolot wrote and directed the documentary *Nefarious: Merchant of Souls* (Grandview, MO: Exodus Cry, 2011), which provides an excellent introduction to the topic of global sex trafficking.

16 Taken originally from Benjamin Nolot, "The Corporatization of Our Sexuality," Benjaminnolot.com (blog), November 1, 2013 (emphasis in original). Nolot shares similar material in Benjamin Nolot, "Contending for Purity in a Pornified World: The Battle for Our Sexuality," The Exodus Cry Blog, September 18, 2013, http://exoduscry.com/blog/general/contending-for-purity-in-a-pornified-world-the-battle-for-our-sexuality/.

17 John Bunyan, *Pilgrim's Progress* (1678; repr., Grand Rapids: Baker, 1984), 175–76.

CHAPTER THIRTEEN: NO CONFIDENCE IN THE FLESH

1 "During the Middle Kingdom, Amun gradually became the chief god of the Theban area, where he acquired a new consort, Mut,

and a son, Khonsu. In the New Kingdom, the cult of Amun was combined with that of the creator sun god Ra. Amun-Ra was worshiped as the King of the Gods and creator of the world and its inhabitants" (Geraldine Pinch, *Egyptian Mythology: A Guide to the Gods, Goddesses, and Traditions of Ancient Egypt* [Oxford: Oxford University Press, 2002], 100).

2 "The National Football League players union, alarmed that its members die nearly 20 years earlier on average than other American men, has selected Harvard University to oversee a $100 million accelerated research initiative aimed at treating and ultimately preventing the broad-ranging health problems plaguing the athletes" (Kay Lazar, "NFL Players Union and Harvard Team Up on Landmark Study of Football Injuries and Illness," Boston.com, January 29, 2013, http://www.boston.com/lifestyle/health/2013/01/29/nfl-players-union-and-harvard-team-landmark-study-football-injuries-and-illness/aCGnf96h7ptWX2Lnp5MIiP/story.html). NFL players know these risks. One NFL player recently said, "My life will revolve around football to some point, but I'd rather have the experience of playing and, who knows, die 10, 15 years earlier than not be able to play in the NFL and live a long life" (John Smallwood, "Is an NFL Career Worth an Early Death?", Philly.com, December 19, 2014, http://articles.philly.com/2014-12-19/sports/57201041_1_nfl-players-association-average-life-expectancy-chris-conte).

CHAPTER FOURTEEN: THE LIBERATION OF NINEVEH

1 Walter Mayr, "Hungary's Peaceful Revolution: Cutting the Fence and Changing History," *Spiegel Online International*, May 29, 2009, http://www.spiegel.de/international/europe/hungary-s-peaceful-revolution-cutting-the-fence-and-changing-history-a-627632-2.html.

2 O. Palmer Robertson, *The Books of Nahum, Habakkuk, and Zephaniah*, The New International Commentary on the Old Testament (Grand Rapids: Eerdmans, 1990), 26.

3 David G. Garber Jr., "Facing Traumatizing Texts: Reading Nahum's Nationalistic Rage," *Review and Expositor* 105, no. 2 (May 2008): 292.

4 Peter C. Craigie, *Twelve Prophets, vol. 2: Micah, Nahum, Habakkuk, Zephaniah, Haggai, Zechariah, and Malachi*, Daily Study Bible Series (Louisville: Westminster John Knox Press, 1985), 61.

5   Kenneth L. Barker and Waylon Bailey, *Micah, Nahum, Habakkuk, Zephaniah*, The New American Commentary 20 (Nashville: Broadman and Holman, 1998), 189.

6   Daniel David Luckenbill, *Ancient Records of Assyria and Babylonia*, vol. 2, *Historical Records of Assyria from Sargon to the End* (Chicago: University of Chicago Press, 1927), 134.

7   George Smith, *History of Assurbanipal, Translated from the Cuneiform Inscriptions* (London: Williams & Norgate, 1871), 34.

8   Each word in Nahum 2:7b exhibits "multi-accentuality," which is "the ability of words and other linguistic signs to carry more than one meaning according to the contexts in which they are used" (Chris Baldick, *The Oxford Dictionary of Literary Terms* [Oxford: Oxford University Press, 2008], 216).

9   Besides the proximity of the two books to each other and the use of each other's names, Jonah and Nahum share three other remarkable similarities. They both focus on the same city. They both quote part of Exodus 34:6–7. They both end with a rhetorical question.

CHAPTER FIFTEEN: THE PRINCE OF DARKNESS

1   Martin Luther, "A Mighty Fortress Is Our God," 1529; trans. Frederick H. Hedge, 1853.

2   "The Code of Hammurabi," in *Ancient Near Eastern Texts Relating to the Old Testament*, ed. James B. Pritchard, 3rd ed. (Princeton: Princeton University Press, 1969), 164.

3   George Smith, *History of Assurbanipal, Translated from the Cuneiform Inscriptions* (London: Williams & Norgate, 1871), 84.

4   Ibid, 103.

5   Ibid, 215.

6   Ibid, 256.

7   Daniel David Luckenbill, *Ancient Records of Assyria and Babylonia*, vol. 2, *Historical Records of Assyria from Sargon to the End* (Chicago: University of Chicago Press, 1927), 273.

8   Michael Burger, *The Shaping of Western Civilization: From Antiquity to the Enlightenment* (Toronto: Broadview Press, 2008), 39.

INDEX OF SCRIPTURE